Check
for teens

Presented To:

_____

Presented By:

_____

Date:

_____

Checklist for Life
for teens

Checklist for Life
for teens

40 Days of Timeless Wisdom
& Foolproof Strategies for
Making the Most of Life's Challenges
& Opportunities

THOMAS NELSON
Since 1798

thomasnelson.com

Scripture quotations noted NKJV are from THE NEW KING JAMES VERSION. Copyright © 1979, 1980, 1982, Thomas Nelson, Inc., Publishers.

Scripture quotations noted CEV are from THE CONTEMPORARY ENGLISH VERSION. © 1991 by the American Bible Society. Used by permission.

Scripture quotations noted GOD'S WORD are from *GOD'S WORD*, a copyrighted work of God's Word to the Nations Bible Society. Quotations are used by permission. Copyright 1995 by God's Word to the Nations Bible Society. All rights reserved.

Scripture quotations noted KJV are from the KING JAMES VERSION.

Scripture quotations noted THE MESSAGE are from *The Message* by Eugene H. Peterson, copyright © 1993, 1994, 1995, 1996, 2000. Used by permission of NavPress Publishing Group. All rights reserved.

Scripture quotations noted NASB are from the NEW AMERICAN STANDARD BIBLE®, © copyright The Lockman Foundation 1960, 1962, 1963, 1968, 1971, 1972, 1973, 1975, 1977, 1995. Used by permission.

Scripture quotations noted NIV are from the HOLY BIBLE: NEW INTERNATIONAL VERSION® copyright © 1973, 1978, 1984 by International Bible Society. Used by permission of Zondervan Publishing House. All rights reserved.

Scripture quotations noted NLT are from the *Holy Bible*, New Living Translation, copyright © 1996. Used by permission of Tyndale House Publishers, Inc., Wheaton, Illinois 60189. All rights reserved.

Scripture quotations noted NRSV are from the NEW REVISED STANDARD VERSION of the Bible, copyright © 1989 by the Division of Christian Education of the National Council of The Churches of Christ in the U.S.A. All rights reserved.

Scripture quotations noted TLB are from *The Living Bible*, copyright © 1971. Used by permission of Tyndale House Publishers, Inc., Wheaton, Illinois 60189. All rights reserved.

Manuscript written and prepared by Marcia Ford
Teen Consultant: Amanda Corn
Design: Whisner Design Group

Previously published as *Checklist for Life for Teens: Timeless Wisdom & Foolproof Strategies for Making the Most of Life's Challenges & Opportunities*

Checklist for life for teens: 40 days of timeless wisdom & foolproof strategies for making the most of life's challenges & opportunities
    p. cm.
ISBN 0-7852-6461-2 (first ed.)
ISBN 10: 0-7852-8892-9 (repak)
ISBN 13: 978-0-7852-8892-3 (repak)
1. Christian teenagers–Religious life. I. Thomas Nelson Publishers.
BV4531.3.C48 2002
248.8'3—dc21

2002006086

Printed in the United States of America

07 08 09 10   RRD   6 5 4 3 2 1

Heart Attitude

I will honor God with my life.

Table of Contents

Introduction 10

Mirror, Mirror (Self-Acceptance) 14

Things Fall Apart (Loss) 20

Exclusive Offer (Cliques). 24

Zero Tolerance (Accepting Others) 28

Choosing Friends (Values) 32

Weight of the Wait (Sex and Intimacy) 36

Why Me? (Purpose) 42

Must-Haves (Instant Gratification) 46

The Ex Files (Handling Breakups) 50

What Do They Know, Anyway? (Parents) 54

Supersize It (Exaggeration) 60

Leader of the Pack (Role Models) 64

Deal with It (Siblings) 68

Gift in Disguise (Consequences). 72

Let's Get Real (Honesty). 78

No One's Looking (Making Ethical Decisions) 82

Zipped Lips (Criticism) 86

Just Do It (Obedience). 90

Ever After (Love) 94

Power Up (Prayer) 100

Making the Cut (Grades and Standards) 104

Instant Replay (Living with Regret) 108

Wanting It All (Jealousy and Envy) 114

Danger Zone (Temptation) 118

Moving Mountains (Overcoming Obstacles) 122

Can't Hurt (Cheerfulness) 126

Go Figure (Handling Money) 130

Wild Blue Yonder (Believing in Yourself) 134

Making a Comeback (Revenge) 138

Don't Sweat It (Choosing Your Battles) 142

The Jury of Your Peers (Peer Pressure) 146

Endless Possibilities (Planning for the Future) 152

Gray Matters (Choices) 156

Cutting Loose (Humor and Laughter) 160

Body Language (Listening) 164

Who's the Boss? (Work) 168

The Real Thing (Spirituality) 172

Mastermind (Self-Control) 176

"Now Be Nice" (Kindness and Compassion) 180

All Grown Up (Maturity) 184

Introduction

Jesus said, "Seek first the kingdom of God and His righteousness, and all these things shall be added to you."—MATTHEW 6:33 NKJV

You are standing on the brink of adulthood, the wide, open spaces of your future spread out before you the way the American West must have looked to the early explorers. The possibilities seem endless and exciting. Others crossed the land before, however, and sent back reports of treacherous mountain passes and spooky canyons, blinding blizzards and tormenting droughts, venomous rattlers and ravenous grizzlies. The breathtaking views from the "purple mountains' majesty" weren't as appealing in fact as they were in imagination.

Take heart. There are safe passages over the land you are about to enter. You can learn to find those passages by preparing yourself in advance, starting right now. What is even better is that you won't have to wait five or ten or twenty years for the payoff, because the discoveries you make will benefit you today, as well as in the future.

This book, like others in the Checklist for Life series, is designed to encourage you on your journey by drawing on the wisdom found in the ultimate travel guide, the

Bible—so keep your Bible nearby. Each overview or insight passage stands alone and focuses on a specific theme. The way you use this book is up to you, working through the book in sequence or reading the entries on specific topics in order of their relevance to your life today. After each passage, reflect on the I Will checklist and perform the actions in the Things to Do checklist. You'll be asked to write some of your thoughts in a journal, so keep a notebook—any kind will do—with your Bible.

Get everything together for your journey: a Bible, a notebook and pen, *Checklist for Life for Teens*, and an open mind and heart. Before you set out, invite God's Spirit to lead you every step of the way. You now have all the equipment you need to get started. Enjoy the journey!

You are not a human being in search of a spiritual experience.
You are a spiritual being immersed in a human experience.
—PIERRE TEILHARD DE CHARDIN

God is the friend of silence. See how nature—trees, flowers, grass—grow in silence? The more we receive in silent prayer, the more we can give in our active life.
—MOTHER TERESA

Everybody can be great. Because anybody can serve... You only need a heart full of grace. A soul generated by love.
—MARTIN LUTHER KING

Let no one despise your youth, but be an example to the believers in word, in conduct, in love, in spirit, in faith, in purity.
1 TIMOTHY 4:12 NKJV

God does not love us because we are valuable. We are valuable because God loves us.
MARTIN LUTHER

I will praise You, for I am fearfully and wonderfully made; marvelous are Your works, and that my soul knows very well.
PSALM 139:14 NKJV

Let us treat men and women well; treat them as if they were real. Perhaps they are.
RALPH WALDO EMERSON

Your ears shall hear a word behind you, saying, "This is the way, walk in it," whenever you turn to the right hand or whenever you turn to the left.
ISAIAH 30:21 NKJV

A loving heart is the truest wisdom.
CHARLES DICKENS

Checklist for Life for teens

The art of contentment is the recognition that the most satisfying and the most dependably refreshing experiences of life lie not in great things but in little.
        —*Edgar Andrew Collard*

I know the thoughts that I think toward you, says the LORD, thoughts of peace and not of evil, to give you a future and a hope.
        —*Jeremiah 29:11 NKJV*

Mirror, Mirror

I will praise You, for I am fearfully and wonderfully made; marvelous are Your works, and that my soul knows very well.

—*Psalm 139:14* NKJV

You are made in the image of God. Hard to believe? You know what it's like to look in the mirror and groan at what you see. Sometimes, the longer you look, the worse it gets! It doesn't help much when your parents tell you that you're just going through a phase, that even the best-looking kids in school think they're ugly or dorky or homely. You see every one of your flaws as clearly as if a huge neon arrow was pointing right at them.

In a way, mirrors distort your true image, especially when you've trained your eyes to see flaws that aren't even there. It's almost as if you're looking into the wavy mirrors in a funhouse—they pull your body this way and that, squish your features, and turn you into a hideous alien from some remote planet. What you need to do is train your eyes to focus on the incredibly wonderful work of God that's staring back at you.

What you think are flaws are often features that simply differ from those of the celebrities you see on television and movie screens and billboards and magazine covers. Are those images typical of reality? No. All you have to do is look around you for one day to realize how few people fit that ideal image. Not everyone can—or, believe it, wants to—look like Mandy Moore or Josh Hartnett. That's a good thing. Think how monotonous and confusing life would be otherwise.

It's the truth: You are made in the image of God, and He has a never-ending supply of features to draw from. He designed every individual in a unique way, right down to the tiniest detail. You can either get mad at God for that, or you can be grateful to Him for caring so much about the way you turned out. Who else has paid you that much attention? Even if anyone else wanted to, no one else could.

In fact, God seems to enjoy lavishing His attention on those who seldom get any. By today's standards, Jeremiah was just a kid when God singled him out to be His spokesman. When Jeremiah objected and pointed out all his flaws, God basically told him to chill. David seems to have been the runt of his family's litter, and he ended up a king. And one Old Testament reference to the Messiah even implies that He— Jesus, that is—wasn't much to look at.

Instead of obsessing over your image in the mirror, try mirroring the image of Jesus, the one that reflects His character. How would you look if you were compassionate toward others and if you went out of your way to help your parents, show kindness to your siblings, and treat everyone equally—even the misfits at your school? You'd start to feel pretty good about yourself, and the way you feel about yourself on the inside always shows up on your face.

Just for today, try thinking about yourself as a new creation. Turn the Golden Rule back on yourself: Do unto yourself as you would have others do unto you! Be good to yourself by refusing to think that you're anything less than terrific. Surround yourself with those friends that make you feel special and significant. Don't even try on the victim role. Laugh right out loud when the mirror tries to tell you you're not the fairest—or handsomest—one of all.

Does all this sound vain? Aren't you supposed to not think all that highly of yourself? Few teenagers, way down deep inside, have a problem with an inflated self-esteem. What the Bible says is that you should not think any more highly of yourself than you ought to. In other words, you need to have an honest, undistorted image of who you are—a unique and cherished person created by the highly creative God. No more than that, of course, but certainly no less than that as well.

Before you were born, God dipped His hand into His limitless well of resources and came up with the precise components He wanted to use to create you. Mirrors do lie, each time they tell you that you're anything less than the very best God has to offer.

I Will

	yes	no
Believe that I am wonderfully made.	_yes_	_no_
Be thankful for the unique features God has given me.	_yes_	_no_
Base my self-image on the image of God.	_yes_	_no_
Surround myself with friends who accept me as I am.	_yes_	_no_
Understand that my friends are also special to God.	_yes_	_no_
Think positive thoughts about myself.	_yes_	_no_
Question negative feedback from my mirror.	_yes_	_no_

Things to Do

☐ Thank God today for the way He made you.

☐ Read Psalm 139 and really think about what it says.

☐ Make a list of your good features. Ask a trusted friend to add to the list.

☐ Catch yourself doing something right today—and smile about it.

☐ Look in the mirror and tell yourself that you are made in the image of God.

☐ Ask God to show you how you can accept yourself completely.

Things to Remember

The Lord said to Samuel, "Do not look at his appearance or at his physical stature, because I have refused him. For the Lord does not see as man sees; for man looks at the outward appearance, but the Lord looks at the heart."

1 SAMUEL 16:7 NKJV

If any man is in Christ, he is a new creature; the old things passed way; behold, new things have come.

2 CORINTHIANS 5:17 NASB

To the praise of the glory of His grace, by which He made us accepted in the Beloved.

—EPHESIANS 1:6 NKJV

Do not judge according to appearance, but judge with righteous judgment.

JOHN 7:24 NKJV

Do not let your adornment be merely outward— arranging the hair, wearing gold, or putting on fine apparel—rather let it be the hidden person of the heart, with the incorruptible beauty of a gentle and quiet spirit, which is very precious in the sight of God.

1 PETER 3:3–4 NKJV

Jesus said to him, "'You shall love the Lord your God with all your heart, with all your soul, and with all your mind.' This is the first and great commandment. And the second is like it: 'You shall love your neighbor as yourself.'"

MATTHEW 22:37–39 NKJV

This precious treasure—this light and power that now shine within us—is held in perishable containers, that is, in our weak bodies.

2 CORINTHIANS 4:7 NLT

Your hands have made me and fashioned me; give me understanding, that I may learn Your commandments.

PSALM 119:73 NKJV

Thus says the LORD, your Redeemer, and He who formed you from the womb: "I am the LORD, who makes all things, who stretches out the heavens all alone, who spreads abroad the earth by Myself."

ISAIAH 44:24 NKJV

The LORD gave me a message. He said, "I knew you before I formed you in your mother's womb. Before you were born I set you apart and appointed you as my spokesman to the world." "O Sovereign LORD," I said, "I can't speak for you! I'm too young!"

JEREMIAH 1:4–6 NLT

God does not love us because we are valuable. We are valuable because God loves us.

—MARTIN LUTHER

Nothing is a greater impediment to being on good terms with others than being ill at ease with yourself.

—HONORÉ DE BALZAC

LOSS

Things Fall Apart

Jesus said, "Come to Me, all you who labor and are heavy laden, and I will give you rest."

—*Matthew 11:28* NKJV

Did you know that you can turn any problem over to God and He will help? Maybe your life has gotten so bad that you wish you could change places with somebody else—in fact, just about anybody else. Maybe your dog had to be put to sleep, or you had to move away from all your friends. Maybe your grandmother died. Maybe your mother or father is so immersed in personal problems that you're being ignored. Maybe your coach had to resign because of serious health problems. Any one of these things could turn your world upside down.

Life-changing situations that involve loss can be dangerous if you don't know how to respond to them. Know that you don't have to go through any of these situations by yourself. You can turn them over to God and lean on Him. The first step in a healthy response to trauma is to admit that you're hurting or that you're angry or that you don't feel like going on. Denying your feelings can set

you up for serious disorders—depression, for example—
and prevent you from getting the help you need.

If you find yourself in an emotionally shattering
situation, immediately turn the problem over to God. By
acknowledging that you have no control over the situation
and that there isn't a thing you can do to change it, you
place yourself in the best position possible to truly let go of
it. Allow God and others to help you handle your loss and
make sense of your life again. Find someone willing to listen
as you vent your feelings—a pastor, a counselor, maybe an
aunt or uncle.

A special word of caution if your loss is related to your
parents' divorce or separation: Don't take responsibility for
their decisions. Don't blame yourself. Don't think you can fix
the problem. Do the most important thing you can do:
Continue to love your parents and pray for God's will to be
done. Place their relationship in God's hands and leave it
there.

Dealing with loss is a process for which there is no
instant cure. A particularly devastating loss can take months
or years to recover from, but as you draw closer to God,
you will begin to feel better much sooner. Make sure you
take a few moments each day to focus on what you still
have instead of what you've lost. In time, you will probably
discover that you wouldn't want to trade places with
anyone else.

I Will

Turn to God to see me through this.   _yes_   _no_

Acknowledge that I have no control over the
situation.   _yes_   _no_

Be thankful for what I still have.   _yes_   _no_

Admit how much I hurt when things fall apart.   _yes_   _no_

Realize that in time, I will begin to feel better.   _yes_   _no_

Understand that there is no instant cure for getting
over a loss.   _yes_   _no_

Things to Do

☐   Ask God to help you handle the loss you've experienced.

☐   Identify what you fear most about the loss you've suffered and give
that fear to God.

☐   Read Psalms 16, 23, 130, and 138.

☐   Go through one day fully alert to all the things you still have.

☐   Write down your thoughts and feelings about loss in a journal.

☐   Find someone to talk to.

Things to Remember

Jesus said, "The Spirit of the Lord is upon Me, because He has anointed me to preach the gospel to the poor; He has sent Me to heal the brokenhearted, to proclaim liberty to the captives and recovery of sight to the blind, to set at liberty those who are oppressed."

LUKE 4:18 NKJV

God, who called you to become his child, will do all this for you, just as he promised.

1 THESSALONIANS 5:24 TLB

Because he has set his love upon Me, therefore I will deliver him; I will set him on high, because he has known My name.

PSALM 91:14 NKJV

The angel of the LORD camps around those who fear God, and he saves them.

PSALM 34:7 NCV

LORD, You have been our dwelling place in all generations.

PSALM 90:1 NKJV

While we may not be able to control all that happens to us, we can control what happens inside us.

BENJAMIN FRANKLIN

Nothing that grieves us can be called little: by the eternal laws of proportion a child's loss of a doll and a king's loss of a crown are events of the same size.

MARK TWAIN

Exclusive Offer

So you may walk in the way of goodness, and keep to the paths of righteousness.

—Proverbs 2:20 NKJV

Anyone who's been in middle school or high school for more than a day knows about cliques—those narrow, exclusive groups of kids who make others feel unwelcome. If you're one of the many who have been banished from a clique, you know how awful that can feel. But being accepted by a clique isn't all it's cracked up to be.

If you're part of a clique now, you need to think carefully about the choice you've made. Most cliques create an imaginary circle around their tight little group and treat everyone outside the circle as if they're diseased. Someone always gets hurt, and the clique acquires a reputation for meanness. And if you have identified yourself with Christ, that's not exactly the kind of reputation you want to have.

In fact, your identity in Christ should be one of the

most important factors you use in deciding if you really want to be a part of any group. A clique tends to take on a personality of its own and homogenize the personalities of its members. You could lose your individuality. Is that really what you want? You as a Christian are a son or daughter of the King; that's an identity worth hanging on to!

The more certain you are of your identity in Christ, the less need you'll have to find your identity in a clique or in anything else. Try to get a clear picture in your mind of who you are in the family of God: an heir of the kingdom, a person of infinite worth, one in whom God's Spirit lives. You have been bought with a price—Jesus' death on the cross—and you belong to God. Jesus is now your friend and your brother. You are holy and acceptable in God's sight, and He says that nothing can separate you from His love. Pretty heady stuff, but that's exactly what your identity in Christ is all about.

Remember this: God extends His kindness beyond the circle of those who identify with Him; His kindness is never exclusive. Make it your goal to so identify with Christ that your acts of kindness extend to those inside and outside the cliques at your school. With your identity firmly established in Jesus Christ, you'll no doubt find it easier to break down those clique-built barriers, one person at a time.

I Will

Consider my identity in Christ before joining any group. _____ yes _____ no

Get a clear picture in my mind of who I am in Jesus Christ. _____ yes _____ no

Allow God to use me to break down the barriers that cliques have built. _____ yes _____ no

Avoid being part of any group that acts superior to others. _____ yes _____ no

Make others feel welcome in my circle of friends. _____ yes _____ no

Extend kindness to others. _____ yes _____ no

Things to Do

☐ Write "I am child of the King" on a piece of paper and place it in your wallet as a reminder of who you are in Christ.

☐ Ask God to reveal any blind spots you have in the way you treat others and resolve to correct the problem by modeling your behavior after Jesus'.

☐ List specific things you can do to show kindness to those outside your immediate circle of friends.

☐ Identify one person you've judged unfairly and carefully attempt to befriend him or her.

☐ Sit next to someone in the cafeteria that you don't normally eat lunch with.

Things to Remember

The LORD said, "You shall do no injustice in judgment. You shall not be partial to the poor, nor honor the person of the mighty. In righteousness you shall judge your neighbor."

LEVITICUS 19:15 NKJV

God created humans to be like himself; he made men and women.

GENESIS 1:27 CEV

My little children, let us not love in word or in tongue, but in deed and in truth. And by this we know that we are of the truth, and shall assure our hearts before Him. For if our heart condemns us, God is greater than our heart, and knows all things.

1 JOHN 3:18–20 NKJV

Are you doing anything remarkable if you welcome only your friends? Everyone does that!

MATTHEW 5:47 GOD'S WORD

Love the stranger, for you were strangers in the land of Egypt.

DEUTERONOMY 10:19 NKJV

We forfeit three-fourths of ourselves in order to be like other people.

ARTHUR SCHOPENHAUER

Three things in human life are important: The first is to be kind. The second is to be kind. And the third is to be kind.

HENRY JAMES

Zero Tolerance

He heals the brokenhearted and binds up their wounds.
—Psalm 147:3 NKJV

Just as Jesus was called to love the seemingly unlovable, so, too, are you. Have you ever known people who seem to have zero tolerance for those who aren't exactly like them? If you don't dress or talk or act the way they think you should, you're a total loser in their eyes, and they let you know it. They treat you as if you've just arrived from another planet and you haven't a clue how earthlings are really supposed to live.

You may not be quite that bad, but if you're like most people you could probably do a better job of accepting those who aren't like you. Sometimes the world seems overrun with misfits, outcasts, loners, and assorted other oddballs, and it can be a challenge to accept them and their eccentric behavior.

God made every one of those oddballs. He allowed His Son to die for them, so He obviously thinks they're valuable. That creates a bit of a problem, doesn't it? It's easy to join in when others make fun of those who are different, and it's hard to stand up for what's right when deep down you think some of those people really are kind of weird. No one is asking you to be best buddies with them. But you are asked to accept and respect them like people who are worth dying for.

People can be annoying and rude and mean. They get on your nerves so much that they drive you up a wall and down the other side. Some are dirty and smell funny and have greasy hair. Are you supposed to love and accept them? Yes—every one of them, just the way Jesus accepted the outcasts of His day. You'll know you're on the path to maturity as a believer when you realize that you're learning to love the unlovable.

You can start by looking at people from a more compassionate perspective. Jesus' compassion toward lepers is a great model for you to follow. He saw them as suffering people in need of a savior, while society treated them as if they were hideous, subhuman life-forms. By embracing the very people that the rest of society shunned, Jesus offered the definitive example of the way He expects His followers to show acceptance of other people. There's no place in His kingdom for people with zero tolerance.

I Will

Appreciate the fact that God made each of us to
be unique individuals.

yes   *no*

Follow Jesus' example of infinite tolerance.

yes   *no*

Realize that making fun of others is based in
ignorance of Jesus' example.

yes   *no*

See every human being as worthwhile and
valuable.

yes   *no*

Be careful of the way I look at those who are
different.

yes   *no*

Be more compassionate toward outcasts.

yes   *no*

Things to Do

☐ Read through the Gospels to see how Jesus treated outcasts like
Zaccheus and Mary Magdalene.

☐ Ask God to reveal to you—and help you overcome—any prejudice in
your life.

☐ Pray for the spiritual maturity to follow Jesus' example and to accept
and respect those who are different from you.

☐ Thank God for accepting you and loving you just the way you are.

☐ Confess any judgmental attitude you may have toward people who are
not like you.

Do not pronounce judgment before the time, before the Lord comes, who will bring to light the things now hidden in darkness and will disclose the purposes of the heart. Then each one will receive commendation from God.

1 CORINTHIANS 4:5 NRSV

Pursue peace with all people, and holiness, without which no one will see the Lord.

HEBREWS 12:14 NKJV

He has shown you, O man, what is good; and what does the Lord require of you but to do justly, to love mercy, and to walk humbly with your God?

MICAH 6:8 NKJV

Jesus said, "Do not judge, so that you may not be judged. For with the judgment you make you will be judged, and the measure you give will be the measure you get."

MATTHEW 7:1–2 NRSV

I charge you before God and the Lord Jesus Christ and the elect angels that you observe these things without prejudice, doing nothing with partiality.

1 TIMOTHY 5:21 NKJV

Let us treat men and women well; treat them as if they were real. Perhaps they are.

RALPH WALDO EMERSON

Let God be as original with other people as He is with you.

OSWALD CHAMBERS

Choosing Friends

Do not be deceived: "Evil company corrupts good habits."
—1 Corinthians 15:33 NKJV

Your choice of friends has greater significance than simply the pleasures of the day. Have you ever wondered why you click with some people and not with others? Sure, you probably have the same interests and look at life in pretty much the same way, but there's more to it than that when it comes to those you call your best friends. There's a connection, something you can't really define. You just click.

That connection, even if you don't talk about it much, is probably based on the values you share. You don't have to sit around all day talking about values to know deep down where your friend stands on important things like honesty and loyalty and trust—the glue that holds your relationship together. When you choose your friends based on positive values, you are living out a principle that is repeated throughout the Bible: You need to choose your friends and companions carefully, since your relationships will in large part determine whether you stay the course of faith.

The Old Testament books of 1 and 2 Samuel offer up one

of the most beautiful examples of friendship in the story of David, the shepherd boy who killed Goliath and eventually became king, and Jonathan, David's brother-in-law and a son of King Saul. These two clicked immediately, and their friendship even survived Saul's attempts to kill David, who had become his archrival for the hearts and allegiance of the people. Jonathan saved David's life by helping him escape Saul's wrath; when Philistine soldiers killed Jonathan, David poured out his grief in a passage called the Song of the Bow (2 Samuel 1:19–27). In it, David placed a higher value on his friendship with Jonathan than on his romantic relationships with women.

The kind of friendship David and Jonathan had is possible today, but it requires a love-based commitment that cannot be shaken by changing circumstances. You can start to develop such a friendship by strengthening your relationships with trustworthy and mature friends who encourage you in your walk with the Lord. Those are the kinds of friends who respect your faith, accept you unconditionally, and motivate you to become a better person than you ever thought you could be.

Place a high priority on maintaining your close friendships; be the one who reaches out and encourages and always gives the benefit of the doubt when misunderstandings threaten the relationship. When you go the extra mile for your friends, you prove yourself to be the kind of friend others want to click with.

I Will

Maintain my values even if my friends trash them.	yes	no
Be a positive influence on my friends.	yes	no
Remain committed to my friends despite the circumstances.	yes	no
Be the kind of friend to others that I would like to have for myself.	yes	no
Be the one to reach out and encourage others.	yes	no
Go the extra mile for my friends.	yes	no

Things to Do

☐ Ask God to show you how you can be a better friend.

☐ Choose a close friend to be a prayer and accountability partner.

☐ Read about the deep friendship between Jonathan and David in 1 Samuel 18–20 and see what you can learn about relationships.

☐ Send an encouraging note or e-mail to a friend who's going through a rough time.

☐ Thank one of your friends for things she's done that helped you.

☐ Make a friendship calendar of specific needs and specific times to be there for your friends.

Things to Remember

The righteous should choose his friends carefully, for the way of the wicked leads them astray.

PROVERBS 12:26 NKJV

Blessed is the man who walks not in the counsel of the ungodly, nor stands in the path of sinners, nor sits in the seat of the scornful.

PSALM 1:1 NKJV

As iron sharpens iron, so people can improve each other.

PROVERBS 27:17 NCV

Ointment and perfume delight the heart, and the sweetness of a man's friend gives delight by hearty counsel.

PROVERBS 27:9 NKJV

The slap of a friend can be trusted to help you, but the kisses of an enemy are nothing but lies.

PROVERBS 27:6 NCV

Many people will walk in and out of your life, but only true friends will leave footprints in your heart.

ELEANOR ROOSEVELT

Friendship is an honest mirror, but it must be allowed to reflect or its power is lost.

MARY HUNT

Weight of the Wait

Do you not know that your body is the temple of the Holy Spirit who is in you, whom you have from God, and you are not your own?

1 Corinthians 6:19 NKJV

By now, you've probably heard the safe-sex message so often that you turn your mind off as soon as you hear the phrase. You've heard all about the potential problems of having unprotected sex, things like disease and unwanted pregnancy. You've also heard all about the various methods people suggest for making sexual activity healthier and safer.

But there's no such thing as safe sex outside of a 100 percent committed marriage relationship. Nothing can keep you safe from all of the consequences of sex before marriage, including a long list of fears. Fear of being found out. Fear of being abandoned by a sexual partner. Fear of genital herpes or AIDS. Fear of pregnancy. Fear that the guilt and shame that weigh you down will never go away.

What's sad is that this is not what God intended when He created this wonderful gift. After all, He's the one who thought all this up, and He wants couples to enjoy it to the fullest. He knows that the way to do that is to hold out for fearless sex, the kind you can only find within the genuinely safe and intimate boundaries of marriage.

Is God asking too much of you? It may seem that way at times, especially if you interpret all the lectures you hear about waiting for marriage as some kind of sadistic punishment to keep you from enjoying physical pleasure. It turns out, though, that God isn't small-minded about sex, people are. God's view of sex is so much bigger and better than the human mind can comprehend. He knows that the true pleasure of the sex act extends beyond the physical into the emotional and spiritual realms, in a way that's downright mysterious.

Some couples try to get around all this by redefining the word *sex*. As long as they don't go all the way, they figure they haven't had sex. They think they can nail their conscience on a technicality. Other couples draw an imaginary line that limits how far they can go, but then they keep moving the line, little by little, until eventually it disappears. Meanwhile, both kinds of couples are playing on a dangerous playground.

Let's get clear on this: Anything that arouses your physical passion in an unhealthy way can be considered too far. For some, this may mean that holding hands and kissing are OK; for others, even that is too much temptation. Regardless, the point should be not to see how far you can go but to learn how to manage your relationship in a way that is totally pleasing to God.

What if you've already blown it? If you're no longer a virgin, all the talk about saving this wonderful gift for your future spouse makes you feel even worse. Well, you have a couple of amazing opportunities before you: You can experience the forgiveness and grace of God on such a deep and awesome level that your life can be changed forever, and you can be there for others who realize too late that they've gone too far.

No matter what your past sexual involvement has been—all or nothing or anything in between—you can start all over today, by settling the issue once and for all. Decide ahead of time how you will handle any and every compromising situation that you may face. Decide that you will not have sex—or engage in any activity that arouses sexual passion—until your wedding night.

This will not be easy. But you can eliminate some of the difficulty by surrounding yourself with like-minded friends who have also made a commitment to sexual purity and to support for each other with prayer and encouragement. You can rest assured that God will help you every step of the way. He always provides an escape route from temptation. He promises that when you focus on your relationship with Him, you can change the way you think and feel about the things that are harmful to you. The more time you spend with Him, the less power today's sexually charged messages will have over you. The more time you spend in His Word, the less confusing those messages will be. And the prospect of having truly safe and fearless sex will make the waiting worthwhile.

I Will

Try to please God in the way I handle my
relationships.   yes ____ no ____

Honor my future marriage partner by waiting to
have sex.   yes ____ no ____

Believe that waiting until marriage is worth the
struggle.   yes ____ no ____

Commit myself to a standard of moral purity.   yes ____ no ____

Guard my mind from impure thoughts about sex.   yes ____ no ____

Focus on my love relationship with God.   yes ____ no ____

Things to Do

☐ Ask God to give you power over sexual temptation.

☐ Memorize helpful scriptures, such as Romans 6:6 and 2 Peter 2:9–10.

☐ Make a commitment to abstinence through the True Love Waits
campaign (www.truelovewaits.com) or a similar, abstinence-based
program.

☐ Find others in your area who have made similar pledges and can help
you live out your commitment.

☐ Write down anything that triggers lustful thoughts (like specific movies
and magazines) and resolve to avoid those things.

Things to Remember

Put to death your members which are on the earth: fornication, uncleanness, passion, evil desire, and covetousness, which is idolatry.

COLOSSIANS 3:5 NKJV

Your old evil desires were nailed to the cross with him; that part of you that loves to sin was crushed and fatally wounded, so that your sin-loving body is no longer under sin's control, no longer needs to be a slave to sin.

ROMANS 6:6 TLB

Put on the Lord Jesus Christ, and make no provision for the flesh, to fulfill its lusts.

—ROMANS 13:14 NKJV

Do you not know that the wicked will not inherit the kingdom of God? Do not be deceived: Neither the sexually immoral nor idolaters nor adulterers nor male prostitutes nor homosexual offenders nor thieves nor the greedy nor drunkards nor slanderers nor swindlers will inherit the kingdom of God.

1 CORINTHIANS 6:9–10 NIV

I have written to you not to keep company with anyone named a brother, who is sexually immoral, or covetous, or an idolater, or a reviler, or a drunkard, or an extortioner—not even to eat with such a person.

1 CORINTHIANS 5:11 NKJV

Don't pour your water in the streets; don't give your love to just any woman.

PROVERBS 5:16 NCV

The way of a guilty man is perverse; but as for the pure, his work is right.

PROVERBS 21:8 NKJV

Flee also youthful lusts; but pursue righteousness, faith, love, peace with those who call on the Lord out of a pure heart.

2 TIMOTHY 2:22 NKJV

The Lord knows how to deliver the godly out of temptations and to reserve the unjust under punishment for the day of judgment.

2 PETER 2:9 NKJV

We have no one to blame but the leering, seducing flare-up of our own lust. Lust gets pregnant, and has a baby: sin! Sin grows up to adulthood, and becomes a real killer.

JAMES 1:14–15 THE MESSAGE

> **Love can always wait to give; lust can never wait to get.**
>
> **—AUTHOR UNKNOWN**

> **Kids are dying from causes of sexual activity. You're not going to find a tombstone stating that Frankie died because he was a virgin.**
>
> **—A. C. GREEN**

Why Me?

The LORD said, "It shall come to pass afterward that I will pour out My Spirit on all flesh; your sons and your daughters shall prophesy, your old men shall dream dreams, your young men shall see visions."

Joel 2:28 NKJV

God put you on earth for a specific reason. Do you wonder what that reason is? You may have a fairly good idea of what kind of work you want to do in the future, but that's a whole different thing. When it comes to your purpose in life—the very reason for your existence—you are talking about something much bigger than any career could ever be. Your purpose is the answer to the question, Why was I born?

This is where things get hairy, because no one else can answer that question for you; you have to discover your unique purpose on your own. A great starting point is the Bible, where you can find some general reasons why you were born. You were made to worship God (Psalm 100); to know Him intimately (Philippians 3:10); to share the Good News of why Jesus came to earth (Matthew

28:9); to help people see God because of your good works (Matthew 5:14 and Ephesians 2:10). These and other verses go a long way toward showing you why on earth you are here.

Still, what is that purpose, specific to you, for which you were born? If you've ever seen *It's a Wonderful Life*, you know what purpose is all about, what life in your world would have been like if you had never been born. George Bailey had a few more years behind him than you do, and you probably won't completely understand your purpose for years to come, if ever. You can get an inkling of it, though, by looking at the lives you've touched in the past and the path you're heading toward in the future. If you're involved in church or a youth group, take a good look at the kind of activities or ministries you tend to gravitate toward. Those activities are huge clues to your purpose in the kingdom of God.

The best resource you have for discovering your purpose, of course, is God Himself. He promises that if you seek His will, you will find it. Ask Him to reveal your specific purpose in life. If you keep a journal, be sure to record any impressions you receive after you've prayed. If you've been keeping a journal for a while, go back and read what God has spoken to you in the past. If you still have trouble finding the answers you're seeking, relax. Keep doing what God has you doing. At just the right time, He'll show you His purpose in your life.

I Will

Believe that God created me for a specific
purpose.   _yes_   _no_

Relax and trust God to reveal my purpose at the
right time.   _yes_   _no_

Remember that my main reason for living is to
love God and be in relationship with Him.   _yes_   _no_

Keep doing what God has me doing right now.   _yes_   _no_

Place my future in God's hands.   _yes_   _no_

Pay attention to the aspects of church life that I
enjoy most.   _yes_   _no_

Things to Do

☐ Ask God to reveal how He wants you to serve Him at this point in your
life.

☐ Write a letter to God asking Him why you were born and where you're
heading. (Be sure to write down any answers He gives you!)

☐ Discover more about your purpose by reading Matthew 6:33, Colossians
3:1–17, Hebrews 10:24–25, Hebrews 13:15, Philippians 2:13, 1 Peter 3:15.

☐ Discover your spiritual gift (1 Corinthians 12) using a test provided by
your church or youth group.

☐ Identify what you enjoy most at church or youth group. Find common
threads to help you discover your purpose.

Things to Remember

Paul wrote: One thing I do, forgetting those things which are behind and reaching forward to those things which are ahead, I press toward the goal for the prize of the upward call of God in Christ Jesus.

PHILIPPIANS 3:13–14 NKJV

In Him also we have obtained an inheritance, being predestined according to the purpose of Him who works all things according to the counsel of His will, that we who first trusted in Christ should be to the praise of His glory.

EPHESIANS 1:11–12 NKJV

God is at work within you, helping you want to obey him, and then helping you do what he wants.

PHILIPPIANS 2:13 TLB

God planned for us to do good things and to live as he has always wanted us to live. That's why he sent Christ to make us what we are.

EPHESIANS 2:10 CEV

Jesus said, "Let your light so shine before men, that they may see your good works and glorify your Father in heaven."

MATTHEW 5:16 NKJV

The only glory which Jesus ever sought for himself or offered to his disciples was to be caught up into God's redemptive purpose.

GEORGE CAIRD

Must-Haves

Jesus said, "Seek first the kingdom of God and His righteousness, and all these things shall be added to you."
—*Matthew 6:33 NKJV*

Waiting and trusting God will put any must-haves in true perspective. But do you have a baby brother or sister? If so, you know what a racket babies make when they want something. They want milk, and they want it now! Giving them what they're demanding now is called instant gratification. They get it almost as soon as they want it. That desire for instant gratification doesn't end when babies graduate from the cradle.

Just like babies, people want to have everything they desire now. You want high-speed Internet access because you need information (OK, downloaded music) now. You have to have a microwave oven because you want your burrito now. You can't wait for spring break or Christmas or the day you get your license or your eighteenth birthday. And that movie you've been dying to see on DVD—well, you can order it online a month before it's released. So what happens when you get it? The high lasts, oh, maybe a day or two. Then, you are on to wanting something else. You're not alone in all this, of course. The desire for instant gratification is quite human.

You don't scream and cry like a baby, but perhaps your attitude may be sometimes just as bad as a baby's when you have to wait for something. The ability to calmly wait for the thing you want so much—called delayed or deferred gratification—is one of the most distinctive indications of a person's maturity. Mature kids are those who have learned to wait, whether it's for their first car or their turn in the spotlight or until marriage to have sex.

The demand for instant gratification also can short-circuit your faith. God has a plan for your life, and He will unfold it as you trust Him. But you also have to trust His timing, and that can mean a whole lot of waiting as He works on bringing you to a place of maturity where He can fulfill His plan.

Denying yourself pleasure or privileges or stuff isn't easy, especially when your friends seem to have it all. But once you've sorted out your genuine needs from the mass of things you feel you must have, you begin to realize that your must-haves aren't all that satisfying. The next time you get that red-hot desire to acquire, call a time-out on yourself. All you may really need is a cooldown period of waiting and trusting God.

I Will

Trust God to provide everything I need.   _yes_   _no_

Learn to cool down and wait on God when I feel I
have to have a certain thing.   _yes_   _no_

Acknowledge my need to accept deferred
gratification.   _yes_   _no_

Rely on God's timing rather than my own.   _yes_   _no_

Find contentment in what I already have.   _yes_   _no_

Bring my impatience under control.   _yes_   _no_

Things to Do

☐ Ask God to help you resist the influence of the now culture in which
you live.

☐ Make a list of your genuine needs and hand the list over to God.

☐ Take an inventory of what you already have—say, all your CDs or
videos. Do you really need more?

☐ Make a list of the things you think you want, cut it in half, then half
again to reduce the list to those things you really want.

☐ Establish a specific waiting period, such as a week or a month, before
you buy anything that is not essential.

☐ Give the clothes you no longer want or wear to a worthwhile charity.

Paul wrote: Not that I speak in regard to need, for I have learned in whatever state I am, to be content.

PHILIPPIANS 4:11 NKJV

Serving God does make us very rich, if we are satisfied with what we have.

1 TIMOTHY 6:6 NCV

Jesus said, "Blessed are those who hunger and thirst for righteousness, for they shall be filled."

MATTHEW 5:6 NKJV

The LORD said, "Why do you spend money for what is not bread, and your wages for what does not satisfy? Listen carefully to Me, and eat what is good, and let your soul delight itself in abundance."

ISAIAH 55:2 NKJV

Command those who are rich in this present age not to be haughty, nor to trust in uncertain riches but in the living God, who gives us richly all things to enjoy.

1 TIMOTHY 6:17 NKJV

Unbridled gratification produces unbridled desire.

TRADITIONAL PROVERB

One sign of maturity is delayed gratification.

PEGGY CAHN

The Ex Files

We are not crushed and broken. We are perplexed, but we don't give up and quit.

—2 Corinthians 4:8 NLT

There's no getting around it: Breaking up is hard to do. Having your heart broken for the first time—when this whole love thing is still so fresh and new—is especially painful. What's worse, everyone knows. You feel like dying, and it seems the whole world is watching.

At times like that, you'd probably like to buy a heart-repair kit. After a few days, you'd be all better, with a fully mended heart and the vague feeling that something kind of bad happened awhile back. The reality is, however, that you were born with a heart that can't be repaired that easily.

What can you do when your heart is broken? Well, you could give up or just give it time. Or you could live a lie, treating your ex as if your relationship never mattered. But that heart you were born with still has a need for love. The hurt and pain may have rearranged things a bit, but your heart is intact.

You may not believe God can touch you, but He can. When you're suffering a deep emotional pain, He takes your heart and smoothes away the bumps and bruises. You have to first give it to Him, trusting that His hands can prepare your heart to love again. When you do love again, you will know more about love than you ever thought possible.

In the meantime, take special care of yourself. Get the rest you need; stay away from caffeine or anything else that interferes with sleep or contributes to depression. Eliminate junk food, which can cause your blood sugar—and emotions—to plummet. Several times a week, go for a walk. You'll feel better all around.

Be careful what—and who—you listen to. You may need to steer clear of the music you normally listen to and find something that will lift your spirits. Although your friends may have good intentions, they can feed your sadness by putting down your ex or passing along news you don't want to hear. It's good to discuss your feelings with a trusted friend, but choose that friend wisely. Make sure you bare your soul to an encouraging friend who can keep a confidence.

Will you ever forget the first time your heart was broken? No. But the pain will diminish as you allow God to start healing your broken heart.

I Will

Give my heart to God to repair.   yes   no

Trust God with my heart in the future.   yes   no

Realize that recovering from a breakup
will take time.   yes   no

Believe that things will get better.   yes   no

Be careful to guard my heart.   yes   no

Be careful with other people's hearts.   yes   no

Treat anyone I've dated with respect.   yes   no

Things to Do

☐ Give your heart to God for safekeeping.

☐ Ask God for wisdom before you give your heart away.

☐ Pray that you'll see God's love for you today.

☐ List qualities (like faithfulness) you require in a person before you
agree to go out with him or her. Resolve not to compromise on those
qualities.

☐ Read Justin Lookadoo's Dateable.

☐ Thank God for His concern for the brokenhearted.

☐ Decide now to always treat an ex with respect.

David wrote: My flesh and my heart fail; but God is the strength of my heart and my portion forever.

PSALM 73:26 NKJV

May the God of hope fill you with all joy and peace in believing, that you may abound in hope by the power of the Holy Spirit.

ROMANS 15:13 NKJV

The LORD is near to those who have a broken heart, and saves such as have a contrite spirit.

PSALM 34:18 NKJV

This is my comfort in my misery: Your promise gave me a new life.

PSALM 119:50 GOD'S WORD

The Lord said, "Then shall the virgin rejoice in the dance, and the young men, and the old, together; for I will turn their mourning to joy, will comfort them, and make them rejoice rather than sorrow."

JEREMIAH 31:13 NKJV

Love is like a violin. The music may stop now and then, but the strings remain forever.

JUNE MASTERS BACHER

Do your utmost to guard your heart, for out of it comes life.

WALTER HILTON

What Do They Know, Anyway?

"Honor your father and mother," which is the first commandment with promise: "that it may be well with you and you may live long on the earth."

Ephesians 6:2–3 NKJV

Wouldn't it be great if you knew someone who could help you sort out everything you're going through right now, someone who could tell you what to expect in the years to come and steer you in the right direction? God always has the wisdom you seek. Sometimes, though, you could use a flesh-and-blood person as a sounding board for the thoughts and ideas and questions that often swirl through your mind.

Well, you do have such a person, or maybe even two—your mother or father or both. Open communication is the key to tapping in to their years of experience and drawing out the wisdom they've acquired. Keeping the lines of communication open is essential to keep things from falling apart at home. And keeping the lines of communication open and clear—without any static on either side—may depend on you more than you realize.

Take a scenario like this: You want to go to college, but you're not sure what you want to do with your life. You'd like to take off a year after high school, work full-time, save some money, and then go to college after you've sorted out your goals. You tell your parents what you're thinking—and your father hits the ceiling. He won't hear of such a plan. You're going to college, and that's that! Your mother has her own concerns, though she reacts by looking away and fighting back the tears. She quietly leaves the room as your father goes on and on about how you'll never get anywhere in life without a college degree. You get mad, because you think he obviously wasn't listening to you in the first place, and you stalk off to your room. The conversation is over. Nothing is settled.

From your perspective, your parents are being downright unreasonable. Well, maybe they didn't handle the situation the way you wish they had, but you have no way of knowing what they were thinking or why they reacted the way they did. You realize that your father never graduated from college—but maybe what you don't know is that he dropped out after two years, figuring he could bum around the country for a while and get his head together. You also realize that your mother never went to college—but maybe what you don't know is that she had always planned to; she just wanted to work for a year after high school and enroll in college later. But then she met your father, and, well, that was the end of college for both of them.

Can you see the dynamics in this scenario from a

different perspective now? Your parents, or rather your hypothetical parents, are trying to spare you the disappointment they experienced because of the questionable choices they made. They want the best for you, and they don't want you repeating their mistakes. And this is exactly why you may need to take the initiative with them. They may not want to think about their failures, let alone share them with you.

So how do you draw on their wisdom? First, make sure your attitude toward them is grounded in respect, which is what honoring your parents is all about. Unless you start from a foundation of respect—treating them with courtesy, always speaking well of them, following their godly example—then your efforts at communication will fall on deaf ears (theirs!). Second, seek God's guidance on the best way, and the best time, to approach them. God is the only one who can see the heart of each person involved, and He can offer insight and practical direction that no one else can.

Third, trust God with the outcome. Maybe your efforts at honest communication will fail. It's even possible that your parents may try to steer you away from what you believe is God's will for your life. Remember this—everyone, including your parents, will eventually disappoint you in some way, just as you will disappoint them. But God never disappoints. When you keep your focus on the primary relationship in your life—the one you have with the Lord—you have the confidence of knowing that the wisdom you seek is as close as He is.

I Will

Honor my parents by showing them respect.

yes   *no*

Turn to my parents for wisdom and guidance.

yes   *no*

Learn to genuinely listen to what my parents are
trying to tell me.

yes   *no*

Realize that my parents are going through
changes too.

yes   *no*

Initiate the process of resolving conflicts with my
parents.

yes   *no*

Express my appreciation to my parents for what
they've done for me.

yes   *no*

Things to Do

☐ Ask God to show you how you can keep communication open with your
parents.

☐ Make a written commitment to treat your parents with the same courtesy
and respect you give to other adults.

☐ List the things that cause problems with your parents (money, curfew,
grades). Next to each item, list what you can do to about those
problems.

☐ Show appropriate physical affection—hug your mother, place your hand
on your father's shoulder.

☐ List all the things your parents provide for you. Be as specific as
possible. Find a way to thank them.

Things to Remember

Hear, my son, and receive my sayings, and the years of your life will be many.

PROVERBS 4:10 NKJV

Endure trials for the sake of discipline. God is treating you as children; for what child is there whom a parent does not discipline?

HEBREWS 12:7 NRSV

Every one of you shall revere his mother and his father, and keep My Sabbaths: I am the Lord your God.

—LEVITICUS 19:3 NKJV

A father of the fatherless, a defender of widows, is God in His holy habitation.

PSALM 68:5 NKJV

Whoever curses his father or his mother, his lamp will be put out in deep darkness.

PROVERBS 20:20 NKJV

Solomon wrote: Hear me now, my children, and do not depart from the words of my mouth.

PROVERBS 5:7 NKJV

Everyone must submit himself to the governing authorities, for there is no authority except that which God has established. The authorities that exist have been established by God.

ROMANS 13:1 NIV

A son honors his father, and a servant his master. If then I am the Father, where is My honor? And if I am a Master, where is My reverence? says the LORD of hosts to you priests who despise My name. Yet you say, "In what way have we despised Your name?"

MALACHI 1:6 NKJV

Even if my father and mother abandon me, the LORD will take care of me.

PSALM 27:10 GOD'S WORD

Keep your father's command, and do not forsake the law of your mother.

PROVERBS 6:20–21 NKJV

Love begins at home, and it is not how much we do but how much love we put in that action.

—MOTHER TERESA

Parents—they're strict on you when you're little, and you don't understand why. But as you get older, you understand and you appreciate it.

—GRANT HILL

EXAGGERATION

Supersize It

In the multitude of words sin is not lacking, but he who restrains his lips is wise.

—*Proverbs 10:19* NKJV

The truth, the whole truth, and nothing but the truth. Right? Your friends surround you, and the spotlight is shining right on you. You're in the middle of telling them this great story about—well, it hardly matters what it's about. You're clearly entertaining them. Suddenly, you get this bright idea that would make the story so much better. So you throw in a couple of details that aren't exactly true, but they sound great. No harm done, right?

Wrong. When you "supersize" your stories, you cross a line from fact into fiction, from truth into untruth. Calling it exaggeration may make it sound better, but it's still a form of lying. Unfortunately, this is a common lapse of integrity among Christians; the phrase "evangelistically speaking" is used in a cynical way to refer to the habit of inflating the number of people at an evangelistic event or the number of decisions for Christ that were logged. Maybe you've even been guilty of a little "evangelistic" exaggeration, thinking you could help out God a bit by adding a few dramatic but untrue touches when you tell others how He's been working in your life lately.

Well, God doesn't need anyone's help. What He needs is for His followers to be people of integrity, people whose word can be trusted. If you habitually exaggerate, you stand to lose your credibility, and that casts a shadow on your reputation as a Christian. How can you be a strong witness for Jesus if others cannot trust what you say? You can't. If you want to share the Good News, your word—your credibility—has to be as good as gold.

Think of it this way: You know you can take God at His word, so people should be able to take you at your word. They shouldn't have to wonder if what you're saying is really true or if you're just off again on another excursion into the land of tall tales. Let the truth of what you're saying stand on its own—you'll only weaken the impact by trying to prop up your words with lies.

When it comes right down to it, supersizing your stories really is a lot like supersizing your fast-food order; it sounds good, but the only thing you get more of is the stuff that's loaded with empty calories. Start downsizing your speech by making sure that every statement you make is true, and forget those bright ideas that sound so good. The truth always makes a better story.

I Will

Remember that God doesn't need me to
exaggerate to make Him sound better.   ___ yes   ___ no

Understand how important credibility is to my
reputation as a Christian.   ___ yes   ___ no

Trust God to help me keep my words pure.   ___ yes   ___ no

Commit myself to complete honesty in my speech. ___ yes   ___ no

Realize that dramatic touches are nothing more
than lies.   ___ yes   ___ no

Focus on maintaining my integrity.   ___ yes   ___ no

Things to Do

☐ Confess the sins of exaggeration you've committed that God's Spirit
brings to your mind right now.

☐ Recall the last time you embellished on a story and figure out what
prompted you to exaggerate.

☐ Pray that God will help you to speak only the truth.

☐ Decide now that next time, you will resist the temptation to supersize
your stories.

☐ Skim a newspaper or magazine until you find an example of
exaggeration and think about how it affects the speaker's or writer's
credibility.

Let no one deceive you with empty words, for because of these things the wrath of God comes on those who are disobedient.

EPHESIANS 5:6 NRSV

There is not a word on my tongue, but behold, O LORD, You know it altogether.

PSALM 139:4 NKJV

"Let him who glories glory in this, that he understands and knows Me, that I am the LORD, exercising lovingkindness, judgment, and righteousness in the earth. For in these I delight," says the LORD.

JEREMIAH 9:24 NKJV

Since you know that he cares, let your language show it. Don't add words like "I swear to God" to your own words. Don't show your impatience by concocting oaths to hurry up God. Just say yes or no. Just say what is true. That way, your language can't be used against you.

JAMES 5:12 THE MESSAGE

The boastful shall not stand in Your sight; You hate all workers of iniquity.

PSALM 5:5 NKJV

We always weaken everything we exaggerate.

JEAN-FRANÇOIS DE LA HARPE

Exaggeration is a blood relation to falsehood and nearly as blamable.

HOSEA BALLOU

Leader of the Pack

Let no one despise your youth, but be an example to the believers in word, in conduct, in love, in spirit, in faith, in purity.
                                        —1 Timothy 4:12 NKJV

When it comes to role models, you've got two considerations to keep in mind: being one and having one. Whether you realize it or not, you are one and you have at least one. That's why it's so important that you understand what a role model is and how a role model influences the lives of others.

People often talk of athletes and celebrities as role models, but the reality is that a genuine role model is someone actively involved in your everyday life, not some distant superstar. Granted, a role model is the kind of person you want to emulate, but a true role model has to be someone you can relate to. It does little good to select a basketball player as a role model if you're barely tall enough to be allowed on the adult rides at Disney World—unless what you're emulating is his character and not his athletic skill. Even so, you'll soon realize that it's the close-at-hand adults in your life—your parents, teachers, youth leader—that will have the greatest effect on your character, because you're constantly observing the way they handle the nitty-gritty details of everyday life. That's a far cry from the media-filtered image that a celebrity wants you to see.

Make no mistake about it, you, too, are a role model, whether for a peer or a sibling or a kid in your neighborhood. No matter what you do, others, particularly younger others, are watching how you handle the ordinary details of everyday life as well. You are having an effect on them, whether for good or for bad. That's another reason why it's critical for you to understand that the words you speak cannot be called back and that the actions you take cannot be erased from the minds and imaginations of others.

Don't ever think that your life is so insignificant that you won't influence someone else. You not only affect the people around you now, but you will also affect generations to come, through your future children. As the saying goes, you may be the only Bible that some people read; the way you live your life stands as a silent witness to your faith in God. That's a daunting thought, but as always, God is right there to take the pressure off. As long as the overriding desire of your life is to please Him, then the influence you have on others can't help but be a positive one.

I Will

Trust God to give me the ability to be a positive
influence on others.
yes   *no*

Understand the influence that those involved in
my daily life are having on me.
yes   *no*

Remember that others are watching
everything I do.
yes   *no*

Be especially careful around younger kids who
may see me as a role model.
yes   *no*

Realize that my life may be the only Bible some
people read.
yes   *no*

Things to Do

☐ List the character qualities that you'd like to emulate and figure out who
in your life models those qualities.

☐ Take that same list and turn it into a set of goals for developing your
own character.

☐ Select a celebrity that you or your friends consider a role model.
Compare what you know about him or her with the character qualities
on your list.

☐ Read a classic on Jesus as the ultimate role model (such as The
Imitation of Christ by Thomas à Kempis, available at
‹http://www.ccel.org/k/kempis/imitation/imitation.html›.

☐ Read about one "radical young believer" from the book Extreme Faith.

Imitate me, just as I also imitate Christ.

1 CORINTHIANS 11:1 NKJV

In everything set [the young men] an example by doing what is good. In your teaching show integrity, seriousness and soundness of speech that cannot be condemned, so that those who oppose you may be ashamed because they have nothing bad to say about us.

TITUS 2:7–8 NIV

Therefore take up the whole armor of God, that you may be able to withstand in the evil day, and having done all, to stand.

EPHESIANS 6:13 NKJV

Paul wrote: Dear brothers, pattern your lives after mine and notice who else lives up to my example.

PHILIPPIANS 3:17 TLB

Your word is a lamp to my feet and a light to my path.

PSALM 119:105 NKJV

There is no power on earth that can neutralize the influence of a high, simple, and useful life.

BOOKER T. WASHINGTON

Nothing is so contagious as an example. We never do great good or evil without bringing about more of the same on the part of others.

FRANÇOIS DE LA ROCHEFOUCAULD

Deal with It

A friend loves at all times, and a brother is born for adversity.

—Proverbs 17:17 NKJV

      Conflicts between siblings are as old as the first post—Garden of Eden society, the family of Adam and Eve. Sibling rivalry turned deadly right away, as Cain killed his brother, Abel, in a fit of jealous rage. In Luke 6, Jesus recommended—rather, commanded—a better way to deal with those people, like siblings, who irritate the daylights out of you: Love them, do good to them, bless them, pray for them. Turn the other cheek so they can hit that one too. Let them steal from you, and give them the shirt off your back. Don't ask them to return what they've taken from you.

      That list probably bugs you, at least a little bit. This isn't easy. You might want to note that Jesus gave no guarantee that the other person's behavior will ever change. He's interested in the changes these actions will make in your character. So don't look for your siblings to act nicer—but then again, don't be all that surprised if the atmosphere at home starts to get a bit more pleasant.

If you don't have a sister or brother, you'll find that these principles also apply to other relationships in your life. In some families, cousins are practically siblings, and the dynamics among cousins can escalate into tension-creating situations similar to what you find among siblings. Like a sister or brother, your cousins will always be related to you, and you share a bond that's not based on preference but on family. God places a great deal of importance on family; it's no accident that you were born into a particular clan. In large part, your personality and character are shaped by the early influences in your life, so you'd do well to learn to appreciate your relatives and treat them in a godly way.

Friends may come and go, but your family will always be your family. As you get older, and especially after you have children of your own, you'll begin to recognize how valuable your family relationships are. Start to treat your siblings as valuable people now, while you're still living at home. Practice kindness and courtesy toward your sister, your brother, your cousin. Look out for them; don't tease or make fun of them, and don't let others do it either. The love you express to your family through your actions will reap untold benefits now and in the future.

I Will

Realize that God is interested in changing my character through my interactions with others.
yes ____ no ____

Believe that Jesus really does want me to treat others as He described in Luke 6.
yes ____ no ____

Appreciate the family God has placed me in.
yes ____ no ____

Treat my siblings and cousins with kindness.
yes ____ no ____

Place a high value on the individual members of my family.
yes ____ no ____

Defend my siblings or other relatives and always speak highly of them.
yes ____ no ____

Things to Do

☐ Thank God for each person in your family, by name.

☐ Identify the main reasons for conflict with your siblings, admit your part in them, and write down what you can do to change.

☐ Read Luke 6 as if Jesus intended for you to take His words seriously.

☐ Who bugs you the most in your family? Make a list of that person's good qualities.

☐ Give your brother or sister or cousin something of value to you, with no strings attached. Make sure you give it out of love and not obligation.

☐ Bless the members of your family by asking God to bless them in some special and specific way.

Whoever loves a brother or sister lives in the light, and in such a person there is no cause for stumbling.

1 JOHN 2:10 NRSV

Behold, how good and how pleasant it is for brethren to dwell together in unity!

PSALM 133:1 NKJV

Jesus said, "Whoever does what God wants is my brother and sister and mother."

MARK 3:35 GOD'S WORD

Jesus said, "The glory which You gave Me I have given them, that they may be one just as We are one: I in them, and You in Me; that they may be made perfect in one, and that the world may know that You have sent Me, and have loved them as You have loved Me."

JOHN 17:22–23 NKJV

May the God of patience and comfort grant you to be like-minded toward one another, according to Christ Jesus.

ROMANS 15:5 NKJV

A brother is a friend provided by nature.

LEGOUVE PEREX

There is no friend like a sister in calm or stormy weather; to cheer one on the tedious way, to fetch one if one goes astray, to lift one if one totters down, to strengthen whilst one stands.

CHRISTINA ROSSETTI

CONSEQUENCES

Gift in Disguise

Do not be deceived, God is not mocked; for whatever a man sows, that he will also reap. For he who sows to his flesh will of the flesh reap corruption, but he who sows to the Spirit will of the Spirit reap everlasting life.

—Galatians 6:7–8 NKJV

If you're not familiar with the story of David and Bathsheba, you might want to take a look at it. It's found in 2 Samuel 11 and 12, and it speaks volumes about the consequences of sin. Briefly, the story goes like this: David notices this woman, Bathsheba, who lives near the palace, and he begins to lust after her. Problem is, she's married. But he's the king, and he generally can get what he wants. So he gets her—and gets her pregnant. Her husband, Uriah, has been off at war, so David sends for him, thinking that Uriah will sleep with Bathsheba. That way, when her pregnancy is discovered, no one will be the wiser; they'll think the baby is Uriah's.

But Uriah turns out to be a principled man—how can he justify engaging in pleasure when the nation is engaged in battle? He makes the mistake of avoiding Bathsheba, so David sends him to the front lines, all but ensuring his death. Uriah is killed, and David takes Bathsheba as his wife. When he is finally convicted of his sin—through the courageous kindness of a man named Nathan—David confesses his sin, repents, and receives God's merciful forgiveness. End of story? No. Look at the consequences of David's sin: Uriah is dead, as is the baby David fathered with Bathsheba. And David's family suffered because of his sin: His daughter, Tamar, was raped by Amnon (her half-brother); his son Absalom killed Amnon; Absalom led an uprising against David and was also eventually killed. According to Nathan, all of this happened because of what David did.

That ought to make you think about the consequences of sin. Even though David was forgiven, he still had to face the tragic events that resulted from caving in to his lustful desires. To his credit, David accepted full responsibility and sought to restore his relationship with God—and he relied on God to help him make the right choices during the turbulent times that followed. The consequence of his sin was a gift that kept his heart turned toward God.

Like David, you need to accept complete responsibility for your sin—along with the consequences. Thinking about those consequences ahead of time can save you a truckload of heartache and trouble in the future. Sin is seldom the isolated act it appears to be; a single act of sin can affect countless people and a host of future decisions. If David could have seen into the future, he no doubt would have hightailed it back into the palace and never stolen another glance at Bathsheba.

Avoiding sin is naturally the best deterrent to suffering

painful consequences. By allowing God to change the desires of your heart, limiting your exposure to tempting opportunities, and exercising self-control when you are confronted with sin, you can avoid following in David's misguided footsteps and possibly taking a lot of other people with you.

Everything you do—even those things that aren't sinful—carries implications. Sometimes you can do more harm than good even when you think you're doing the right thing. Peter did that, as did the Galatian church, and they both got quite a talking to from Paul. In their zeal, they had placed pressure on new believers and added legalistic rules to the gospel. Paul set them straight, but there's no telling how many potential converts were turned off before he got wind of the problem.

Learning to think before you act is not a bad habit to get into. Neither is asking yourself that once-trendy-but-still-valid question, "What would Jesus do?" You can't expect to accurately predict what will happen, but by fast-forwarding your thoughts into the future, your imagination can do a pretty good job of offering up a series of possible scenarios. By looking to Jesus as the ideal example of living right, you should have a lot less concern about the consequences of the decisions you make.

Because of the disobedience of Adam and Eve in the Garden of Eden, we live in a sinful world. Because of the obedience of Christ on the cross, we will have a sin-free eternity. The consequences of those two events affected billions of people and the decisions they made.

I Will

Ask "What would Jesus do?" when I'm not sure
how to decide.   *yes*   *no*

Realize that everything I do has implications.   *yes*   *no*

Accept full responsibility for my actions.   *yes*   *no*

Learn to think before I act.   *yes*   *no*

Avoid every opportunity for sin that I
possibly can.   *yes*   *no*

Understand that I can do harm even when I think
I'm doing something right.   *yes*   *no*

Things to Do

☐ Ask God to help you think about the consequences of your actions
before you act.

☐ Read Daniel 6 from the perspective of Daniel's obedience.

☐ Read Acts 5:1–11 to discover the consequences of Ananias's and
Sapphira's disobedience.

☐ Mentally replay your day to see how the decisions you made affected
the way the day went.

☐ Pray for someone whose poor choices have had negative consequences
in your life.

Things to Remember

God saw how corrupt the earth had become, for all the people on earth had corrupted their ways. So God said to Noah, "I am going to put an end to all people, for the earth is filled with violence because of them. I am surely going to destroy both them and the earth."

GENESIS 6:12–13 NIV

I, the Lord, search the heart, I test the mind,
Even to give every man according to his ways,
According to the fruit of his doings.

JEREMIAH 17:10 NKJV

Beloved, if our heart does not condemn us, we have confidence toward God. And whatever we ask we receive from Him, because we keep His commandments and do those things that are pleasing in His sight.

—1 JOHN 3:21–22 NKJV

To Adam, God said, "Because you listened to your wife and ate the fruit when I told you not to, I have placed a curse upon the soil. All your life you will struggle to extract a living from it."

GENESIS 3:17 TLB

Peter said to Simon, "Your money perish with you, because you thought that the gift of God could be purchased with money! You have neither part nor portion in this matter, for your heart is not right in the sight of God."

ACTS 8:20–21 NKJV

The wages of sin is death, but the gift of God is eternal life in Christ Jesus our Lord.

ROMANS 6:23 NKJV

Jesus said, "He who receives a prophet in the name of a prophet shall receive a prophet's reward; and he who receives a righteous man in the name of a righteous man shall receive a righteous man's reward. And whoever in the name of a disciple gives to one of these little ones even a cup of cold water to drink, truly I say to you, he shall not lose his reward."

MATTHEW 10:41–42 NASB

Be sure to give to [the poor] without any hesitation. When you do this, the Lord your God will bless you in everything you work for and set out to do.

DEUTERONOMY 15:10 GOD'S WORD

Daniel said, "My God sent his angel to shut the lions' mouths so that they would not hurt me, for I have been found innocent in his sight. And I have not wronged you, Your Majesty." The king was overjoyed and ordered that Daniel be lifted from the den. Not a scratch was found on him because he had trusted in his God.

DANIEL 6:22–23 NLT

Sooner or later everyone sits down to a banquet of consequences.

—ROBERT LOUIS STEVENSON

Every act is an act of self-sacrifice. When you choose anything you reject everything else.

—G. K. CHESTERSON

HONESTY

Let's Get Real

Therefore, putting away lying, "Let each one of you speak truth with his neighbor," for we are members of one another.

—Ephesians 4:25 NKJV

Imagine what it would be like if you went to school tomorrow and discovered that you didn't recognize a single person. A few of your friends might seem a bit familiar, but they just didn't look the same. You'd feel as if you were dreaming, or were having a nightmare, or were the victim of some cruel hoax. But that imaginary scene at your school is what life would be like if you and everyone else removed their masks for a day.

Everyone wears a mask—the image they want others to see. What does yours look like? If it looks pretty much like the real you, you're among the minority. Many people wear masks that bear little resemblance to the real person behind it. What makes their lives so sad is that in their efforts to put on a good face for other people, they destroy any possibility of genuine fellowship with the very people they hope to impress.

By pretending to be someone or something you're not, you are undermining the work of God in your life. He made you the way you are. He loves you the way you are, but other people can't. How can they, if you never show them the real you? How will you ever know if their love and acceptance is genuine? If all they ever see is this phony image you've been presenting, you will never have the confidence of knowing that they accept you for who you really are.

Presenting a false image is a form of dishonesty, one that deceives other people and destroys your self-esteem. It's also among the greatest hindrances to open fellowship among Christians. Jesus came not only to reconcile humanity to God but also to reconcile person to person. When you place a false image between your true self and your fellow believers, you build a barrier.

Let people see the real you. Make yourself transparent and vulnerable to other Christians, even though it means that you'll run the risk of getting hurt. Honor the work of God in your life by stripping away the mask—or the many masks—you've been wearing. You'll become more approachable, more accessible, and more likable to others. And you might start to like yourself a little bit more as well.

I Will

Realize that I am undermining God's creation when I try to be something I'm not.

yes _____ no _____

Show my real self to other people.

yes _____ no _____

Appreciate the person I am inside.

yes _____ no _____

Recognize those times when I am most likely to put on a mask.

yes _____ no _____

Make myself vulnerable and transparent to other believers.

yes _____ no _____

Try to get to know the real person behind the mask another person is wearing.

yes _____ no _____

Things to Do

☐ Ask God to reveal to you the various masks you wear (such as a "perfect Christian" mask).

☐ Hand over to God your fear of exposing the real you.

☐ Ask God to give you the strength to drop your masks and be the person He made you to be.

☐ Ask yourself what's the worst that could happen if you removed your masks.

☐ Read Acts 2:42–47 for a glimpse at how the early believers fellowshipped with each other.

He who would love life and see good days, let him refrain his tongue from evil, and his lips from speaking deceit.

1 PETER 3:10 NKJV

As long as my breath is in me and the spirit of God is in my nostrils, my lips will not speak falsehood, and my tongue will not utter deceit.

JOB 27:3–4 NRSV

Jesus said, "You shall know the truth, and the truth shall make you free."

JOHN 8:32 NKJV

David wrote: He who works deceit shall not dwell within my house; he who tells lies shall not continue in my presence.

PSALM 101:7 NKJV

A righteous man hates lying, but a wicked man is loathsome and comes to shame.

PROVERBS 13:5 NKJV

No man, for any considerable period, can wear one face to himself, and another to the multitude, without finally getting bewildered as to which may be true.

NATHANIEL HAWTHORNE

The easiest thing to be in the world is you. The most difficult thing to be is what other people want you to be. Don't let them put you in that position.

LEO BUSCAGLIA

MAKING ETHICAL DECISIONS

No One's Looking

Lord, who may abide in Your tabernacle? Who may dwell in Your holy hill? He who walks uprightly, and works righteousness, and speaks the truth in his heart.

—*Psalm 15:1–2 NKJV*

God's Spirit talks to you through your conscience. Consider this scenario: It's late, you've had a rough day, and you're mindlessly chatting away with your buddies over the Internet. You get distracted by a pop-up window and just as mindlessly click on an innocuous-looking link. That's when your eyes just about pop out of your head. The image that appears is... indescribable in print. You quickly try to close the window, and six more like it suddenly appear on the screen. As you start to close each window, you find that your "clicker" is losing steam. You're not as quick at closing those windows as you were at first. But it's OK; there's no real harm done. No one's looking, right? Right?

Wrong, of course. For one thing, you are. You're looking at pictures that appeal to your worst instincts, and your conscience is sending out danger signals. And God is looking. He's not going to strike you down—though He has been known to do that kind of thing—but He is grieving at your willful sin. He's not holding you accountable for seeing that first image, but as for the ones that followed—well, that's another story. And that's the heart of unethical behavior—engaging in willful sin, particularly under circumstances that make it unlikely that you'll get caught.

In a single day, you may have dozens of occasions to make ethical decisions, most of which you handle without much thought. Maybe your guidance counselor has left you alone in her office for five minutes, just enough time for you to take a peek at some juicy files. But you don't even think twice about that—and you've scored an ethical victory without even realizing it.

Your conscience is your closest ally in your efforts to live an ethical life, because it's through your conscience that God's Spirit lets you know when you're about to cross over into questionable or dangerous territory. Think of the way your conscience has operated up until now. Has it ever given you wholehearted permission to sin along with a guarantee that you wouldn't be found out? No. Your conscience doesn't wink at you and look the other way so you can do something you know is wrong.

Become a God-pleaser by choosing to do right whenever you're confronted with an ethical dilemma—even when you think no one's looking. As you well know, someone always is.

I Will

Thank God for His mercy when I've made bad decisions in the past.

<u>yes</u>   <u>no</u>

Realize that the Bible offers clear guidance for godly behavior.

<u>yes</u>   <u>no</u>

Trust the Spirit of God to lead me to make ethical decisions.

<u>yes</u>   <u>no</u>

Do the right thing, even in private.

<u>yes</u>   <u>no</u>

Pay attention to what my conscience is telling me.

<u>yes</u>   <u>no</u>

Think less about getting caught and more about pleasing God.

<u>yes</u>   <u>no</u>

Things to Do

☐ Make a commitment to God to adhere to a biblical standard of ethical behavior. Write it down.

☐ Meditate on the psalms that deal with ethical behavior, like Psalms 1, 15, and 37.

☐ Think back over the past week and mentally assess how you handled questionable circumstances.

☐ Prepare a defense against situation ethics—the belief that an action can be either right or wrong depending on the situation.

☐ Ask God to forgive you for the times you have willfully disregarded your conscience.

Let integrity and uprightness preserve me, for I wait for You.

PSALM 25:21 NKJV

If we forgot the name of our God or stretched out our hands to pray to another god, wouldn't God find out, since he knows the secrets in our hearts?

PSALM 44:20–21 GOD'S WORD

When Gentiles, who do not have the law, by nature do things in the law, these, although not having the law, are a law to themselves, who show the work of the law written in their hearts, their conscience also bearing witness, and between themselves their thoughts accusing or else excusing them.

ROMANS 2:14–15 NKJV

Create in me a clean heart, O God, and renew a steadfast spirit in me.

PSALM 51:10 NKJV

O Lord, You have searched me and known me. You know my sitting down and my rising up; you understand my thought afar off.

PSALM 139:1–2 NKJV

Evangelical faith without Christian ethics is a travesty on the gospel.

V. RAYMOND EDMAN

Let us raise a standard to which the wise and honest can repair; the rest is in the hands of God.

GEORGE WASHINGTON

CRITICISM

Zipped Lips

Do not speak evil of one another, brethren. He who speaks evil of a brother and judges his brother, speaks evil of the law and judges the law. But if you judge the law, you are not a doer of the law but a judge. There is one Lawgiver, who is able to save and to destroy. Who are you to judge another?

—*James 4:11–12 NKJV*

Critic or criticizer? You had a really great time at a concert. You and your friends blew all your money on tickets and food, but it was worth it. On the way home, you couldn't stop talking about what a terrific show the band put on; you couldn't wait to tell the others kids about it. But the next day, hunched over a bowl of cereal, you read a review of the concert in the local paper. What? This guy slammed the sound system, thought the music was inane, and called the band a bunch of Backstreet wanna-bes! Who does he think he is?

Critics—they're everywhere. Even staring back at you in the mirror. The only real difference is that professional critics get paid to judge the way people perform, while amateur critics—everybody else—do it for free. You don't think you're critical? Some people are plagued by a critical spirit, and maybe you're not that bad. But if you're a living, breathing human, you do pass judgment on people and the things they do, and some of it is undoubtedly unfair. Even if you manage to zip your lips, your critical attitude is still there. But there's really good news for anyone (like you!) who wants to change his or her judgmental ways.

Like most negative traits, the tendency to criticize has a positive counterpart, and that's where the good news comes into play. A critical person often has great ideas for the best way to get things done. When you feel the urge to criticize the activities your youth group is planning or the way the decorations are turning out for your school's homecoming, all you have to do is resist the temptation, roll up your sleeves, and get to work. You have a much-needed contribution to make.

Whenever you find yourself criticizing individuals, however, a signal should go off in your head alerting you to the fact that this is a Golden Rule moment. That should stop your critical thoughts dead in their tracks. And remember this: To apply the Golden Rule as found in Matthew 7:12, you can't just avoid treating another person badly—you have to treat the person well, the way you'd like to be treated.

Most people know the Golden Rule, but few actually live by it. Be the first one on your block to follow it. Zip your lips, allow God to change your attitude, and turn your critical thoughts into an opportunity to do good to others.

I Will

Depend on God to help me change my negative
attitudes.   _yes_   _no_

Turn my criticisms into opportunities to do good.   _yes_   _no_

Practice living by the Golden Rule.   _yes_   _no_

Keep my critical thoughts to myself.   _yes_   _no_

Help out when I see people doing something that
could be done in a better way.   _yes_   _no_

Realize that although everyone judges other
people, I can control my critical thoughts.   _yes_   _no_

Things to Do

☐ Write out the Golden Rule and list the ways you can apply it to your
family members, your friends, and your teachers and church leaders.

☐ Ask God to help you conquer your judgmental nature.

☐ Meditate on Jesus' words in Matthew 7:1–12.

☐ List other positive counterparts to criticism, like discernment. Make a
commitment to developing those character traits.

☐ Volunteer to work on a project you've been critical of.

☐ Write a positive review of one of your church's projects.

Jesus said, "Therefore, whatever you want men to do to you, do also to them, for this is the Law and the Prophets."

MATTHEW 7:12 NKJV

Jesus said, Judge not, and ye shall not be judged: condemn not, and ye shall not be condemned: forgive, and ye shall be forgiven.

LUKE 6:37 KJV

Let us not judge one another anymore, but rather resolve this, not to put a stumbling block or a cause to fall in our brother's way.

ROMANS 14:13 NKJV

Who are you to criticize God? Should the thing made say to the one who made it, "Why have you made me like this?"

ROMANS 9:20 TLB

Jesus said, "Why do you look at the speck in your brother's eyes, but do not consider the plank in your own eye? Or how can you say to your brother, 'Let me remove the speck from your eye'; and look, a plank is in your own eye? Hypocrite! First remove the plank from your own eye, and then you will see clearly to remove the speck from your brother's eye."

MATTHEW 7:3–5 NKJV

Any fool can criticize, condemn and complain—and most do.

DALE CARNEGIE

OBEDIENCE

Just Do It

All these blessings shall come upon you and overtake you, because you obey the voice of the Lord your God.
—Deuteronomy 28:2 NKJV

Jon's boss—Mr. Mac Donald—thought Jon was a model employee at Mac's burger franchise. Jon seemed to do his job with relish. But when Big Mac wasn't around, which was often, Jon slacked off, bullying the rest of his crew—mostly younger high-school students—with disturbing threats. His unsuspecting boss promoted him to franchise manager.

Across the street, Cynthia worked after school at a pet store owned by a man who was messier and smellier than the living inventory. She swore that the next time he barked at her to clean the puppies' cages, she was going to bark right back. But when the next time came, who was in the store but Dustin Timberline, the coolest guy in town. Instead of barking, Cynthia smiled sweetly as she glanced at Dustin on her way to scoop out the—um, stuff—from the cages.

A mile away, Kerry swept the floor of the beauty shop for the nth time. "Go clean the restroom!" the manager ordered. It's

OK, she thought, brushing off Janet's clipped manner. She's stressed over the lack of business. Cleaning the restroom will give me a chance to pray for her in private.

Three obedient employees, right? They all did what they were told to do; technically they all obeyed. But only Kerry met God's definition of genuine obedience—a submissive attitude of the heart coupled with immediate action.

Can you see the differences in the way Jon, Cynthia, and Kerry complied with the demands of their jobs? Jon's obedience was limited and was motivated by selfishness; Cynthia's obedience was motivated by Dustin's presence—she was afraid of looking bad in front of him. But Kerry's obedience was motivated by love—if not for Janet, then for her ultimate boss, God Himself.

Genuine love is the key to genuine obedience. If you love God, you will obey Him. If you love God, you will also follow His command to obey your parents and anyone else in authority over you. But remember: His brand of obedience requires a major heart adjustment; no more obeying on the outside while rebelling on the inside.

Your unquestioned obedience to the will of God will bring you a measure of joy and peace that you simply can't experience when you're living in disobedience. The earlier you learn that, the better. Just wait a while and ask Jon and Cynthia—because eventually, a disobedient spirit can't help but show its ugly face to the world.

I Will

Understand that ultimately, God is my boss.

       yes   _no_

Have an attitude of immediate obedience to those in authority over me.

       yes   _no_

Be thankful for the authority figures that God has placed in my life to protect and instruct me.

       yes   _no_

Make sure my obedience is motivated by love.

       yes   _no_

Expect my obedience to produce joy and peace.

       yes   _no_

Decide to take advantage of unpleasant tasks by praying through them.

       yes   _no_

Things to Do

☐ Repent of your disobedience toward God and others, and accept His forgiveness.

☐ Ask God to change your heart and give you an obedient spirit.

☐ Read through one of the Gospels to learn from Jesus' example of obedience to the Father.

☐ Memorize Matthew 7:21.

☐ Pray for those in authority over you.

☐ Discover what motivates your obedience by paying close attention to the way you react to authority figures for the next few days. Make sure at least one day is a school day or a work day.

Whoever resists the authority resists the ordinance of God, and those who resist will bring judgment on themselves.

ROMANS 13:2 NKJV

Solomon wrote: My father also taught me, and said to me: "Let your heart retain my words; keep my commands, and live."

PROVERBS 4:4 NKJV

Jesus said, "Not everyone who says to Me, 'Lord, Lord,' will enter the kingdom of heaven, but he who does the will of My Father who is in heaven."

MATTHEW 7:21 NASB

The time has come for judgment to begin at the house of God; and if it begins with us first, what will be the end of those who do not obey the gospel of God?

1 PETER 4:17 NKJV

Through Christ, God gave me the special work of an apostle, which was to lead people of all nations to believe and obey. I do this work for him.

ROMANS 1:5 NCV

Obedience to God is the most infallible evidence of sincere and supreme love to him.

NATHANAEL EMMONS

I find the doing of the will of God leaves me no time for disputing about His plans.

GEORGE MACDONALD

Ever After

Keep your heart with all diligence, for out of it spring the issues of life.

—*Proverbs 4:23* NKJV

This is finally it—you've met the one! He's popular, he's handsome, he takes you nice places and makes your heart flutter; she's beautiful and sweet and irresistible, and she has this great laugh. And you both love the Lord! What could be better?

Plenty, starting with a couple of no-brainers, like having God's seal of approval on your relationship and basing your attraction on something other than superficial traits. If you want a love that's going to last "ever after," you need to understand a few things.

Romantic love is without a doubt one of the coolest of God's gifts. It brings out the best in you if you handle it carefully. It makes all your senses come alive, almost to the point of overload. Like all of God's gifts, however, this one can be abused. When it is, it leaves devastated lives in its wake. So before you take the plunge into a love-drenched relationship, back off the edge and pay attention to what God has to say about this awesome gift.

Start with His repeated admonitions, first to the Israelites and then to the early church, to avoid becoming entangled with anyone outside the family of faith. Maybe your intended has memorized hundreds of Bible verses and never misses a youth group meeting. To put it bluntly, that doesn't mean a thing. What do you know of her private relationship with God? What are his spiritual hopes and dreams for the future? How do you relate to God as a couple?

The answers to those and other questions are critical, because marriage is the hardest blessing you'll ever have (until the kids come, but that's another story altogether). Marriage? Where did that come from? You're just talking about being in love! But if you're not ready to think seriously about marriage, you're not ready to fall in love. Why not? Because if the relationship isn't leading toward marriage, you're just toying with another person's heart. You're in love with the idea of being in love, and the shine wears off of that really fast.

Before you go checking out potential mates, take a look at some of the qualities God suggests you look for; they may surprise you. Did you know that young women are encouraged to seek a man who treats animals well, has compassion for the poor, and makes sound business decisions? Those qualities probably aren't on your Ideal Husband list. And guys—when you go pursuing a wife, place a low priority on her beauty, make sure she fears the Lord, and run in the opposite direction if she's argumentative! These and other characteristics of a suitable mate are all found in the book of Proverbs—a great place to spend a lot of time if you're thinking about marriage.

After you've done all that, you still need to trust God completely in this area of your life. That's difficult when your heart is doing somersaults; you're afraid that if you let this one go, there's no telling what God's going to come up with. You love Him and all, but you worry that He might be a bit lacking in the taste department. But who knows what you need better than God does? Who better understands what you desire in a mate? Who wants you to have a successful marriage more than God does? He won't hook you up with someone you can't stand to look at for an evening, let alone the rest of your life. Remember, He loves you—and torture is not an aspect of love.

Avoid serious relationships until you're ready for marriage; meanwhile, socialize in a crowd or with different groups of friends. Don't confuse physical attraction with love; get a clear idea of the inner qualities you want in a mate and don't compromise on them. Never, ever expect the person to change. What you see is what you're going to get, not some improved version you hope to create. Hold out for that one who cherishes you, treats you like gold, and allows you to be yourself. Focus on being the right person instead of finding the right person. Most of all, trust God to give you wisdom and discernment and peace of mind about your decision.

I Will

Trust God's timing when it comes to getting involved in a serious relationship.

yes _____ *no* _____

Hold out for God's best when it comes to love and marriage.

yes _____ *no* _____

Learn to rely more on a person's inner qualities than on his or her outward appearance.

yes _____ *no* _____

Limit the field of potential mates to those on the same spiritual wavelength I'm on.

yes _____ *no* _____

Focus on being the right person for the one I will eventually marry.

yes _____ *no* _____

Things to Do

☐ Ask God to work in the life of your future mate, even though you may not know who that is and marriage could be a decade or more away.

☐ Ask God to use this time in your life to prepare you to be the right kind of mate.

☐ Make a list of all the characteristics you want in a mate. Pray over it, refine it according to God's leading, and entrust it to His care until the time is right.

☐ Now go through the book of Proverbs and write down the desirable characteristics of a husband and a wife. Compare them with those on your ideal-mate list and your own character.

Do not be unequally yoked together with unbelievers.
For what fellowship has righteousness with lawlessness?
And what communion has light with darkness?

2 CORINTHIANS 6:14 NKJV

Those who live following their sinful selves think only
about things that their sinful selves want. But those who
live following the Spirit are thinking about the things the
Spirit wants them to do.

ROMANS 8:5 NCV

Houses and riches are an inheritance from fathers, but
a prudent wife is from the LORD.

—PROVERBS 19:14 NKJV

Charm is deceitful and beauty is passing, but a woman
who fears the LORD, she shall be praised.

PROVERBS 31:30 NKJV

The Shulamite said: Let him kiss me with the kisses of
his mouth—for your love is better than wine.

SONG OF SOLOMON 1:2 NKJV

Jacob served seven years for Rachel, and they seemed only a few days to him because of the love he had for her.

GENESIS 29:20 NKJV

A time to love, and a time to hate; a time of war, and a time of peace

ECCLESIASTES 3:8 NKJV

Young women of Jerusalem, swear to me by the gazelles or by the does in the field, that you will not awaken love or arouse love before its proper time.

SONG OF SOLOMON 3:5 GOD'S WORD

Love never stops being patient, never stops believing, never stops hoping, never gives up.

1 CORINTHIANS 13:7 GOD'S WORD

Love is strong as death, passion fierce as the grave. Its flashes are flashes of fire, a raging flame.

SONG OF SOLOMON 8:6 NRSV

Unfailing love and truth have met together. Righteousness and peace have kissed!

PSALM 85:10 NLT

Two souls with but a single thought, Two hearts that beat as one.

—**FRANZ JOSEPH VON MÜNCH-BELLINGHAUSEN**

Whoso loves believes the impossible.

—**ELIZABETH BARRETT BROWNING**

PRAYER

Power Up

Confess your trespasses to one another, and pray for one another, that you may be healed. The effective, fervent prayer of a righteous man avails much.

—James 5:16 NKJV

Suddenly, your palms are sweaty, your mind's a blank, your mouth won't move, and you can't find your voice. No, you haven't just seen the most beautiful creature on God's green earth—you've just been asked to say the closing prayer at your youth group meeting. Or how about this: You're the only one in the house. No one's expected home for hours. You kneel on the floor, figuring that now you'll be able to pray. But as the words come out, you feel self-conscious. You wonder if anyone is listening—including God!

If that's you, take heart. Lots of Christians talk a big talk about the importance of prayer, but few admit (or seem to remember) how difficult it can be, especially when you haven't had a whole lot of practice. You need some pointers to get you started, and there's no better place to start than the Bible.

Take a look at the Lord's Prayer. You're not expected to use those exact words, though there's nothing wrong with that. Jesus gave you His prayer as a model for your own: acknowledging who God is, desiring His will to be accomplished on earth, asking for basic needs, seeking forgiveness and deliverance, and praising Him. You can't go wrong praying along those lines. As long as you avoid making it personal, this is a good way to pray in public.

You can also try praying the psalms. Many individual psalms were written as prayers to the Lord. Find those that express what's in your heart and pray them back to God. Since some psalms are intensely personal, save this for your private times of prayer. Find other scriptures you can pray back to God. "Lord, You say in Your word that where two or three are gathered, You are in their midst, so we believe You are with us now." Or, "Lord, according to Your word, if I confess my sins, You will be faithful to forgive me and lead me into righteousness." Depending on the scripture you choose, you can use this method for both public and private prayer.

There's nothing wrong with practicing in private until you're comfortable with public prayer. But never forget this: God is longing to hear you express to Him what's in your heart. Your eloquence is meaningless. What counts is the genuine love and faith behind your words, no matter how simple they may be.

I Will

Trust God to help me overcome my discomfort
with prayer, both public and private.

_yes_____ _no_____

Give God my fear when I pray publicly and my
self-consciousness when I pray privately.

_yes_____ _no_____

Realize that prayer is simply a matter of talking
with God.

_yes_____ _no_____

Pray in my own way, avoiding pompous,
eloquent—sounding words that I don't
normally use.

_yes_____ _no_____

Understand that the more I pray, the easier
it will get.

_yes_____ _no_____

Things to Do

☐ Study the Lord's Prayer and use it as a model to create your own
personal variation.

☐ Find a dozen psalms that you can memorize over time and pray back to
God.

☐ Create a special notebook to keep with your Bible for copying verses
that you can later pray back to God.

☐ Write down what you'd like to say to God in prayer. (There—you've
just prayed!)

☐ Read Fuel: Igniting Your Life with Passionate Prayer.

Things to Remember

Be anxious for nothing, but in everything by prayer and supplication, with thanksgiving, let your requests be made known to God.

PHILIPPIANS 4:6 NKJV

The LORD said, "It shall come to pass that before they call, I will answer; and while they are still speaking, I will hear."

ISAIAH 65:24 NKJV

Jesus said, If ye shall ask any thing in my name, I will do it.

JOHN 14:14 KJV

Jesus said, "Whatever things you ask when you pray, believe that you receive them, and you will have them."

MARK 11:24 NKJV

The Lord said, "If My people who are called by My name will humble themselves, and pray and seek My face, and turn from their wicked ways, then I will hear from heaven, and will forgive their sin and heal their land."

2 CHRONICLES 7:14 NKJV

Prayer is not overcoming God's reluctance; it is laying hold of His highest willingness.

RICHARD CHENEVIX TRENCH

Let prayer be the key of the day and the bolt of the night.

JEAN PAUL RICHTER

Making the Cut

To give prudence to the simple, to the young man knowledge and discretion.

—*Proverbs 1:4 NKJV*

Grades—doesn't it seem as if your life revolves around them? If you're planning to go to college, your high school records are reduced to initialisms like GPA and SAT whose numbers determine which college will admit you and which scholarships you qualify for. Or if you're an "average" student—whatever that means—people don't expect much from you, forgetting that some of the most successful people in the world got straight C's all through high school and never even went to college.

If grades are the standard by which you gauge your potential to succeed, you're in trouble! Generally, your academic years are the only ones in which your grades will count for anything. Once you get out into the work world, no one will care how many times you made the honor roll or whether you failed geometry—unless, of course, you've been hired as an engineer, architect, math teacher, or the like. Does that mean you shouldn't strive to get good grades? No. You should always do your best and attempt to excel in whatever you do.

What will count in the years to come and in your future career are your character—who you are on the inside—and your ability to apply what you've learned in school to your life and to your work. You may think that the first will determine how well you succeed as a person and the second will determine how well you succeed in your career. But you'd be mistaken. Your character determines both kinds of success.

You can set unrealistic standards for the kind of grades you'd like to get, but you can never set your moral, ethical, and spiritual standards too high. You may be a solid D student when it comes to math but a straight A student when it comes to loving God and treating others with compassion and fairness and placing a high value on integrity. Which set of grades will matter for eternity?

If your parents are pressuring you to get better grades, you need to do your best to meet their expectations by working hard and relying on God to help you. If you're putting excessive, impossible pressure on yourself, stop. Making the academic cut is not worth it—making the eternal cut is. If you're going to put pressure on yourself, be sure it counts for something worthwhile—like living right while you're on earth and spending eternity with God.

I Will

Trust God to help me excel in whatever I do.

Stop thinking of grades as predictors of my chances for success in the future.

Realize that my character will help determine how well I succeed in my career.

Focus on developing high moral, ethical, and spiritual standards.

Let up the pressure on myself to meet unrealistic academic demands.

Things to Do

 Ask God to show you which character traits you need to improve and thank Him in advance for the help He'll give you in making those improvements.

Ask God for the strength and power to adhere to the standards you've set for your life.

Read through one of the Gospels and write down everything you learn about Christ's character.

List the ways you can apply what you've learned about Jesus to your own character standard.

Rate your spiritual life by giving yourself grades in subjects like time alone with God, Bible reading and study, prayer, obedience, and so forth. See where there's room for improvement.

"Who has known the mind of the Lord that he may instruct Him?" But we have the mind of Christ.

1 CORINTHIANS 2:16 NKJV

The soul of a lazy man desires, and has nothing; but the soul of the diligent shall be made rich.

PROVERBS 13:4 NKJV

Be diligent to present yourself approved to God, a worker who does not need to be ashamed, rightly dividing the word of truth.

2 TIMOTHY 2:15 NKJV

Be doers of the word, and not hearers only, deceiving yourselves.

JAMES 1:22 NKJV

Jesus said, "I can guarantee that unless you live a life that has God's approval and do it more faithfully than the scribes and Pharisees, you will never enter the kingdom of heaven."

MATTHEW 5:20 GOD'S WORD

For us, with the rule of right and wrong given us by Christ, there is nothing for which we have no standard.

LEO TOLSTOY

Ah, but a man's reach should exceed his grasp,
Or what's a heaven for?

ROBERT BROWNING

Instant Replay

He will not dwell unduly on the days of his life, because God keeps him busy with the joy of his heart.
—*Ecclesiastes 5:20 NKJV*

Notice the faraway look that some adults get when they're talking to you about your life. You're having a seemingly normal conversation with your uncle about your plans to go to college, and suddenly he looks off into the distance, nodding his head at the right moments but clearly not really with you anymore. Or you're telling your cousin about this guy you've been dating and how you figure you'll get married right after high school—and you realize your aunt is just within hearing distance, looking at you with a hint of sadness in her eyes. Your aunt and uncle are probably mentally replaying something in their past that they'd rather forget.

What you see in their eyes is regret—a deep and profound sorrow for the poor decisions in their past. Your uncle regrets not going to college; your aunt regrets getting married too soon. When they say they wish they could be seventeen again, it's not because they had such a great time as teenagers. It's because they'd like to have the opportunity to make better decisions, especially the ones that would affect the course of their lives for decades to come.

Living with regret creates an indescribably sad existence. As a teenager, you are in an incomparable position to make the right decisions in life, since most of the major decisions you'll have to make are still ahead of you. As a Christian, you're in the best position of all, because you have access to God's wisdom and the peace of mind He gives when you've made the right decision. Commit your future, with its myriad life-altering decisions, to God, and you'll never have to learn to live with regret.

Maybe, though, you've already made some serious mistakes that you wish you hadn't. While you can't go back and change the situation or its consequences, you can pick yourself up, brush yourself off, and get on with your life. But before you do, you'd be wise to spend a little time in the book of Acts with the apostle Paul.

If anyone had a good reason to regret the things he'd done in his life, it was Paul. He was an accomplice in the murder of Stephen, the first Christian martyr—if not as a stone-thrower, then at least as a cheering spectator. He persecuted Christians at every turn and was proud of it. Imagine how he must have felt when the Lord brought him to his knees and showed him how very wrong he was. But Paul had the good sense not only to fully accept Jesus' free gift of complete and unconditional forgiveness, but also to fully forgive himself for the poor choices he had made. Can you do that—completely accept God's forgiveness and forgive yourself? If you can, you're on your way to living a regret-free life.

One word of caution: When you go to God to express your sorrow over the things you've done, examine your heart first to be sure yours is a godly sorrow. What is it that you regret—getting caught or disappointing God? What are you truly experiencing—embarrassment in the presence of other people or repentance in the presence of God? Whenever you go to God hoping to experience forgiveness, you must go in total integrity, willing to expose your sinful heart to Him so He can replace it with a clean heart.

Do you still have regrets? The good news is that many decisions can be reversed; you can get off the wrong path that you've been taking through your decisions and start walking on the right path that God is wanting you to take. Have you made a decision that can't be reversed? There's good news in that situation as well. Though you'll have to live with the consequences, God can free you from living with regret if you'll only trust Him to lavish His wisdom and His joy on you.

Stop replaying the mental tapes of the mistakes you've made; all those instant replays will only make you miserable. Learn to live in the present as Paul did, by forgetting the past and pressing on to the future. When you let go of regret, you can face the coming years with excitement and expectancy for what God has in store for you.

I Will

Trust God to help me make decisions that I won't
regret later.   yes   no

Realize that the things I do today will play a part
in shaping my life for years to come.   yes   no

Face the future with excitement and expectancy.   yes   no

Learn to live in the present.   yes   no

Reverse a bad decision as soon as I realize I've
made one.   yes   no

Stop mentally replaying the mistakes I've made.   yes   no

Things to Do

☐ Resolve to seek God's wisdom and the counsel of others for the life-
changing decisions you'll face in the coming years.

☐ Read an account of Paul's life before and after his dramatic conversion
to see how he was able to erase any regret for the sins of his past.

☐ Memorize Isaiah 43:18–19 or another verse on the next two pages. Better
yet, memorize all of them!

☐ Make a poster for your bedroom that reads: "Will I regret this decision
in the future?"

☐ Help a friend let go of the regret they're wallowing in.

If we confess our sins, He is faithful and just to forgive us our sins and to cleanse us from all unrighteousness.

1 JOHN 1:9 NKJV

The weapons of our warfare are not carnal but mighty in God for pulling down strongholds, casting down arguments and every high thing that exalts itself against the knowledge of God, bringing every thought into captivity to the obedience of Christ.

2 CORINTHIANS 10:4–5 NKJV

Be renewed in the spirit of your mind.

—EPHESIANS 4:23 NKJV

How far has the LORD taken our sins from us? Farther than the distance from east to west.

PSALM 103:12 CEV

Do not remember the former things, nor consider the things of old. Behold, I will do a new thing, now it shall spring forth; shall you not know it? I will even make a road in the wilderness and rivers in the desert.

ISAIAH 43:18–19 NKJV

He has made everything beautiful in its time. Also He has put eternity in their hearts, except that no one can find out the work that God does from beginning to end.

ECCLESIASTES 3:11 NKJV

A voice from heaven said, "God will wipe away every tear from their eyes; there shall be no more death, nor sorrow, nor crying. There shall be no more pain, for the former things have passed away."

REVELATION 21:4 NKJV

Godly sorrow brings repentance that leads to salvation and leaves no regret, but worldly sorrow brings death.

2 CORINTHIANS 7:10 NIV

Repent therefore and be converted, that your sins may be blotted out, so that times of refreshing may come from the presence of the Lord.

ACTS 3:19 NKJV

Sing, O heavens! Be joyful, O earth! And break out in singing, O mountains! For the Lord has comforted His people, and will have mercy on His afflicted.

ISAIAH 49:13 NKJV

Go to the effort. Invest the time. Write the letter. Make the apology. Take the trip. Purchase the gift. Do it. The seized opportunity renders joy. The neglected brings regret.

—MAX LUCADO

Nobody who ever gave his best regretted it.

—GEORGE HALAS

Wanting It All

Let us not become conceited, provoking one another,
envying one another.

—*Galatians 5:26* NKJV

Your buddy Dave got the most incredible cherry-red
sports car over summer vacation, and you could hardly
stand to be around him whenever he started talking about
it. But that was nothing compared to the way you felt
when Nick—the guy who stole your girlfriend last year—
drove up in a brand-new four-wheel drive. Him, you
wanted to clobber. You secretly hoped his Jeep would be
repossessed and they'd reopen debtor's prison just for his
sorry self.

So what's the verdict here on your bad-attitude
charges? Guilty of one count of jealousy, in the matter of
your buddy Dave. Guilty of one count of jealousy and one
count of envy, in the matter of your sorry enemy Nick. In
both matters laid out before the godly court, you wanted
something you couldn't have, something that belonged to
someone else. That's jealousy. Think of it as a
misdemeanor, something of a lesser charge. But in the

matter of Nick, you also wanted to do him bodily harm and deprive him of his wheels, all four of them. This is a more serious charge, closely akin to a felony.

Now that you're a spiritually convicted felon, what will you do about it? Plead before the court for mercy, of course. And God will forgive you and extend His mercy to you. But it's your responsibility to deal with the root problem: wanting it all. Not only the sports car and the four-wheel drive but also the pain and suffering of a guy named Nick. Give it up. You'll never have it all. You'll never even have most of it all. So plead with the court for one more favor, the gift of contentment. That's another gift that God will gladly give you; be prepared to accept it.

The irony here is that in one sense, you already have it all—everything you need in life, in the person of Jesus Christ. So maybe you can't use Him to impress your friends as you drive around town. But His light shining through your life will draw the right kind of onlookers, those whose hearts are aching for the kind of love He offers.

Jealousy and envy threaten to destroy your relationships, rob you of peace and joy, and keep your focus glued to material things. Godly contentment takes your eyes off of things and returns your focus where it belongs: on God and the people around you who need to see the light of Christ in your satisfied life.

I Will

Keep my focus on God and those who need to see
His love through me.   yes ____   no ____

Allow others to see the light of Christ in me by
giving up my jealous and envious feelings.   yes ____   no ____

Understand that I have everything I need in the
person of Jesus Christ.   yes ____   no ____

Expect God to show me how to be content with
what I have.   yes ____   no ____

Begin to repair the relationships I've damaged by
my bad attitudes.   yes ____   no ____

Things to Do

 Confess your feelings of jealousy and envy to God.

 Read the story of Joseph and his brothers in Genesis 37 for an eye-
opening account of the kind of behavior that jealousy and envy can
lead to.

☐ Think of a recent incident that stirred up jealous feelings within you.
Decide how you could have handled the situation in a more mature way.

☐ Memorize Hebrews 13:5.

☐ There's a positive side to jealousy. Read about it in 2 Corinthians 11:2–3.

Let your conduct be without covetousness; be content with such things as you have. For He Himself has said, "I will never leave you nor forsake you."

HEBREWS 13:5 NKJV

Love suffers long and is kind; love does not envy; love does not parade itself, is not puffed up.

1 CORINTHIANS 13:4 NKJV

The effects of the corrupt nature are obvious: illicit sex, perversion, promiscuity, idolatry, drug use, hatred, rivalry, jealousy, angry outbursts, selfish ambition, conflict, factions, envy, drunkenness, wild partying, and similar things. I've told you in the past and I'm telling you again that people who do these kinds of things will not inherit the kingdom of God.

GALATIANS 5:19–21 GOD'S WORD

You are still carnal. For where there are envy, strife, and divisions among you, are you not carnal and behaving like mere men?

1 CORINTHIANS 3:3 NKJV

Envy takes the joy, happiness, and contentment out of living.

BILLY GRAHAM

They that envy others are their inferiors.

AUTHOR UNKNOWN

TEMPTATION

Danger Zone

We do not have a High Priest who cannot sympathize with our weaknesses, but was in all points tempted as we are, yet without sin. Let us therefore come boldly to the throne of grace, that we may obtain mercy and find grace to help in time of need.

—Hebrews 4:15–16 NKJV

Ah, what a great morning! You wake up in time to get dressed, eat a really good breakfast, and even spend a few minutes in prayer and Bible reading. You grab your schoolbooks and head for the front door. You turn the knob, the door opens, and you step outside. But watch out! You've just entered the Danger Zone.

Day in and day out, you're surrounded by temptation, even if the inside of your house has been swept clean of every influence that could tempt you to sin. Once you step outside, it's as if you're in the middle of the North Atlantic, with icy mountains of temptation scattered across the horizon. In the course of a single day, you'll have more opportunities to lie, cheat, and steal than you ever thought possible. And that's just the tip of the iceberg. The pile of hidden temptations is big enough to sink the *Titanic*.

Fortunately, you're stronger than the *Titanic* if you remember to give your day, with all its temptations, to God when you pray each morning. And if you've been faithful to stay in close contact with the Father all throughout the day, then you have such a sensitive radar system that you can spot the iceberg of sin looming in your path in plenty of time to change your course. You also have the wisdom to know that the icebergs will always be out there, and an immediate course correction is the only way to avoid them.

Maybe you're not such a great navigator yet. All this is so new to you. How on earth—or on sea—can you handle the myriad temptations in your way? You learn from the Master, the one who stood on a mountaintop and stared temptation down. With each temptation that Satan offered Him, Jesus struck a devastating blow, quoting from the Word of God. "It is written," He said, reciting a definitive verse from the scriptures. Satan could not withstand the truth. He left Jesus alone and took his bag of sinful temptations with him.

Temptation is unavoidable. The way you handle temptation is what will make the difference in your spiritual track record. With some really fast running shoes and an arsenal of memorized scripture, you can flee temptation and wage a verbal counterattack at the same time. With each victory you'll build up your resistance to temptation and no longer fear the moment you have to step out into the Danger Zone.

I Will

Remember to give my day to God each morning.
     ___ yes   ___ no

Place a high priority on memorizing scripture so I'll
be prepared for Satan's attacks.
     ___ yes   ___ no

Flee temptation as soon as I recognize it.
     ___ yes   ___ no

Realize that I cannot avoid temptation, but I can
avoid giving in to it.
     ___ yes   ___ no

Trust God to make me sensitive to the first signs of
temptation.
     ___ yes   ___ no

Learn how to resist Satan by following Jesus'
example.
     ___ yes   ___ no

Things to Do

☐ Read the account of Jesus' temptation by Satan in Matthew 4.

☐ Identify the greatest temptations in your life right now. Eliminate anything that feeds that temptation (certain videos, for instance).

☐ Memorize 1 Corinthians 10:13. It's a great verse to remember when you're tempted. (Remember to look for the way of escape!)

☐ Post a reminder—someplace where you're sure to see it each morning— to ask God to help you resist temptation.

☐ Recall the last time you gave in to temptation. See if you can now identify the "way of escape" God had provided for you.

Things to Remember

Jesus said, "Watch and pray, lest you enter into temptation. The spirit indeed is willing, but the flesh is weak."

MARK 14:38 NKJV

Ponder the path of your feet, and let all your ways be established. Do not turn to the right or the left; remove your foot from evil.

PROVERBS 4:26–27 NKJV

How can a young man cleanse his way? By taking heed according to Your word.

PSALM 119:9 NKJV

No testing has overtaken you that is not common to everyone. God is faithful, and he will not let you be tested beyond your strength, but with the testing he will also provide the way out so that you may be able to endure it.

1 CORINTHIANS 10:13 NRSV

Humble yourselves before God. Resist the Devil, and he will flee from you.

JAMES 4:7 NLT

Most people who fly from temptation usually leave a forwarding address.

AUTHOR UNKNOWN

Temptation is the fire that brings up the scum of the heart.

THOMAS BOSTON

Moving Mountains

Jesus said, "I say to you, if you have faith as a mustard seed, you will say to this mountain, 'Move from here to there,' and it will move; and nothing will be impossible for you."

—*Matthew 17:20* NKJV

Maybe you've heard the tale about the ancient king who placed a boulder in the middle of a road. Everyone took the long way around it, all the while complaining about the king's failure to maintain the highways, until a lowly peasant came along and pushed the boulder out of the way. Where the boulder had been he found a purse filled with gold coins, a gift from the king intended for the person who removed the boulder. The moral of the story? Every obstacle offers the possibility of improving your lot in life.

What about you? Are you like the complainers who take the long way around an obstacle? Or are you like the one person who removed the obstacle and found a better life in its place? Maybe you don't think you have the strength to move the boulders that are blocking your path right now, but you know the One who does. And He once said that if you have even the tiniest measure of faith, you can move mountains. A boulder is nothing to Him!

Genuine faith in God is an overcoming faith. It's a faith that does not make a U-turn when it faces a boulder in the road, nor does it take the long way around. It's a faith that knows how to cut to the chase, because faith in God is an active faith that gets things done. It's the kind of faith that enables an elderly woman to bear a child, breaks down prison doors so the captives can go free, and renders the bite of a venomous snake completely harmless—just three of the many accounts of overcoming faith found in the Bible.

No matter what is standing in your way right now, God is big enough to remove it. And He'll do it, if the way you're traveling is the course He has set you on. If the boulder between you and college is tuition, trust Him to provide the funds at just the right time. Maybe the biggest obstacle in your life is failure to communicate with your parents. Trust God; He invented communication. Can't find a job? God loves work! Trust Him to lead you to the right job.

Are you getting the picture? The way to overcome obstacles is by activating your faith in God. Take whatever measure of faith you have right now and trust God to move the boulder in your life. In its place, you just may find a life-changing treasure.

I Will

Trust God to remove the obstacles in my life.   *yes* _____   *no* _____

Focus on God, not on the obstacles.   *yes* _____   *no* _____

Learn to see obstacles as opportunities.   *yes* _____   *no* _____

Make sure I'm on the right path when I call on
God to move the boulder in my way.   *yes* _____   *no* _____

Realize that even the smallest amount of faith can
accomplish great results.   *yes* _____   *no* _____

Be thankful for the opportunities I have to activate
my faith.   *yes* _____   *no* _____

Things to Do

- [ ] Read the accounts of overcoming faith mentioned in Genesis 21, Acts 16, and Acts 28.

- [ ] Identify the biggest obstacle in your life right now. Give it to God and imagine Him rolling it out of your path.

- [ ] Memorize Matthew 17:20.

- [ ] Meditate on what it means to activate your faith.

- [ ] Thank God for giving you the kind of faith that can move mountains.

- [ ] Write an account of all the obstacles God has removed from your life so far.

Things to Remember

Whatever is born of God overcomes the world. And this is the victory that has overcome the world—our faith.

1 JOHN 5:4 NKJV

Even the youths shall faint and be weary, and the young men shall utterly fall, but those who wait on the LORD shall renew their strength; they shall mount up with wings like eagles, they shall run and not be weary, they shall walk and not faint.

ISAIAH 40:30–31 NKJV

It has become evident to the whole palace guard, and to all the rest, that my chains are in Christ; and most of the brethren in the Lord, having become confident by my chains, are much more bold to speak the word without fear.

PHILIPPIANS 1:13–14 NKJV

In all these things we overwhelmingly conquer through Him who loved us.

ROMANS 8:37 NASB

He did not say, "You shall not be tempted; you shall not be travailed; you shall not be afflicted." But he said, "You shall not be overcome."

SAINT JULIAN OF NORWICH

The Promised Land always lies on the other side of a wilderness.

HAVELOCK ELLIS

CHEERFULNESS

Can't Hurt

All the days of the afflicted are evil, but he who is of a merry heart has a continual feast.

—Proverbs 15:15 NKJV

Here's a good one for you: Go through whatever teen or young adult magazines you have lying around the house and try to find an advertisement featuring a cheerful model. Warning: This may take some time. In fact, this may be Mission Impossible. For whatever reason, adopting a defiant, pouty, or just plain miserable attitude has become chic. The worst offenders are rock bands, including some Christian groups. Check out the CD covers—does anyone appear to be even slightly happy, let alone joyful? What's baffling is that when you see these same performers in concert or on a talk show, they're clearly enjoying themselves.

Now that you know that their trendy attitude is all a put-on, you can breathe a sigh of relief and stop trying to conform to the false image they've been conveying. Constantly wearing an expression of gloom and doom can eventually deceive you into believing that your life really is gloomy and doomed. So ditch the pouty persona and start telling yourself the truth, that it's OK to be cheerful. Look at it this way: It can't hurt. And you have an awful lot to be cheerful about.

One surefire way to transform your countenance into a cheerful one is to start singing praises to God. Go ahead—you can do it! If you've never sung praises to God on your own before, it might feel awkward at first. But once you've done it for a while, you'll become so comfortable with it that you'll be hearing praise songs in your head while you're at school or playing basketball or flipping burgers. And you know what? The joy that's in your spirit will show on your face.

Wouldn't you like to be known as a person who can light up a room just by entering it? That sounds so enchanting; it's the type of compliment that you believe should be reserved for the likes of Julia Roberts. Your smile may not be as big as hers, but it can still light up a room. And it can create a healthy buzz about you: What's her secret? they'll start asking, or How can he be so pleasant all the time? You know the answer. What better way to tell others about Jesus?

Your face reflects the condition of your heart. If your heart isn't joyful, there's a problem in your relationship with God. Ask Him how to fix it—and be prepared to do a whole lot of smiling when the repair work is over.

I Will

Remind myself that my cheerfulness is a positive witness for Christ.

___yes___   ___no___

Be more cheerful in my attitude and my appearance.

___yes___   ___no___

Ignore the chic trend to appear defiant.

___yes___   ___no___

Realize that the expression on my face reflects the condition of my heart.

___yes___   ___no___

Cultivate a joyful heart.

___yes___   ___no___

☐ Smile. Right now. For no reason at all.

☐ Ask God to help you be more cheerful.

☐ Make a list of the praise songs you know. Keep the list in your Bible so you'll never be at a loss for a song to sing.

☐ Write a letter to a Christian band asking why their CD covers don't reflect the joy of knowing Jesus. Send the letter. Rejoice if you get a response!

☐ Memorize Proverbs 15:15. After all, who doesn't like food?

☐ For the next three days, be cheerful whenever you're around your parents.

Praise the LORD! Praise the LORD, O my soul! While I live I will praise the LORD; I will sing praises to my God while I have my being.

PSALM 146:1–2 NKJV

Anyone who is having troubles should pray. Anyone who is happy should sing praises.

JAMES 5:13 NCV

When you eat the labor of your hands, you shall be happy, and it shall be well with you.

PSALM 128:2 NKJV

Every man according as he purposeth in his heart, so let him give; not grudgingly, or of necessity: for God loveth a cheerful giver.

2 CORINTHIANS 9:7 KJV

Praise the LORD! Praise, O servants of the LORD, praise the name of the LORD! Blessed be the name of the LORD from this time forth and forevermore! From the rising of the sun to its going down the LORD's name is to be praised.

PSALM 113:1–3 NKJV

Health and cheerfulness mutually beget each other.

JOSEPH ADDISON

Hope is the power of being cheerful in circumstances we know to be desperate.

G. K. CHESTERTON

#

My God shall supply all your need according to His riches in glory by Christ Jesus.

—Philippians 4:19 NKJV

It's tough being a teenager and listening to adults talk about how money can't buy happiness and how you need to be frugal and how you shouldn't strive to be wealthy. After all, you've never even had any real money, just pocket change at best.

They don't lay off because they know that they'd be doing you a disservice. Most adults know that if you learn to handle money when you're young, you have a greater shot at handling it well for the rest of your life. That's what you want, isn't it? The things they're advising you to do now will pay off in the future. You've probably heard it all: Tithe religiously. Give freely. Spend cautiously. Save abundantly. Invest carefully. Budget regularly. It's all good advice. But these are just starting points.

What you need to do is develop a healthy attitude toward money. Money can be your servant or your master, and you get to choose which one it will be. Let's say you make the right choice and decree that money will be your servant from now on. Now you're on a roll. Your servant is there to meet your needs and to help finance God's work. Your servant enables you to live a life of contentment and joy and never threatens to usurp God's place in your life.

If you allow money to become the master of your life, watch out! You'll never have enough. You'll waste your life worrying about how much you have and how much you want to have and how to keep it secure. Since you can't serve two masters, there goes your opportunity to serve God. You'll end up buying things, things, and more things to try to restore the joy you once knew in the presence of God. All that stuff will rob you of time and energy, as you dust it, clean it, maintain it, repair it, store it, display it, and move it from house to house for the rest of your life. Pretty depressing prospects for the future, wouldn't you say?

You can handle your money wisely and still have fun with it, as long as you keep it in its position of servitude. Let your money work for you and for God. Be a good steward of your finances today—even if your assets total only $3.52, safely tucked away in a piggy bank.

I Will

Place a high priority on God's work when it comes
to spending my money.   _yes_   _no_

Avoid financial disaster by drawing on God's
wisdom and the advice of others.   _yes_   _no_

Allow God to have control over my finances.   _yes_   _no_

Make money my servant and not my master.   _yes_   _no_

Develop a healthy attitude toward money.   _yes_   _no_

Find contentment in life, not in things.   _yes_   _no_

Things to Do

☐ Officially make God the master of your finances. Ask Him to give you
wisdom for the financial decisions you have to make.

☐ Look up the word stewardship using an online study Bible and read the
corresponding verses.

☐ Keep a log of how much money you spend in a week. Don't forget all
those coins you feed to vending machines.

☐ The following week, try to break your record by spending less.

☐ Count up all the money you have right now. Tithe on it, even if your
tithe only amounts to 35 cents from that piggy bank of yours.

God is the one who gives seed to the farmer and then bread to eat. In the same way, he will give you many opportunities to do good, and he will produce a great harvest of generosity in you. Yes, you will be enriched so that you can give even more generously. And when we take your gifts to those who need them, they will break out in thanksgiving to God.

2 CORINTHIANS 9:10–11 NLT

A good man leaves an inheritance to his children's children, but the wealth of the sinner is stored up for the righteous.

PROVERBS 13:22 NKJV

In the Parable of the Talents, Jesus said, "Well done, good and faithful servant; you have been faithful over a few things, I will make you ruler over many things. Enter into the joy of your lord."

MATTHEW 25:23 NKJV

The love of money is at the root of all kinds of evil. And some people, craving money, have wandered from the faith and pierced themselves with many sorrows.

1 TIMOTHY 6:10 NLT

When I have any money I get rid of it as quickly as possible, lest it find a way into my heart.

JOHN WESLEY

Money spent on myself may be a millstone about my neck; money spent on others may give me wings like the angels.

ROSWELL DWIGHT HITCHCOCK

Wild Blue Yonder

God has not given us a spirit of fear, but of power and of love and of a sound mind.

—*2 Timothy 1:7* NKJV

There you are, sitting in your guidance counselor's office for the umpteenth time, listening to her talk about how you're college material and you have all this potential and what a waste it would be if you didn't at least give it a try. *I don't know*, you're thinking. *Maybe she's right. But I just don't think I could cut it at college. I'm not sure I have what it takes.* Time will tell whether you have what it takes, but right now it's pretty obvious what you don't have: a healthy measure of self-confidence.

There's no valid reason for a Christian to lack confidence. Sure, you shouldn't walk around acting as if you can conquer the world and crush everybody in it, but neither should you doubt your own abilities. You're not only a precious human being made in the image of God, you're also a spiritually regenerated person, which simply means you've been born again into the family of God. You really can do all things through Christ who strengthens you.

Just watch out when people try to convince you that you can be anything you want to be. That's, well, a lie. It simply is not true. Believing in yourself doesn't mean that you can be a world-famous doctor if you can't stand the sight of blood, or a top-notch lawyer if you hate to argue in defense of an issue. You'll only experience frustration if you believe in yourself without believing in the One who created you and following the path He has chosen for you. He knows you better than you know yourself, and He will lead you to become the person He knows you can be.

If you're having problems with self-confidence, you probably need to hand over your self-esteem to God. He's the expert at those kinds of repairs, and He'll have you believing in yourself in no time. He wants your self-esteem to be healthy, because He knows you'll never meet your spiritual potential until it is.

From now on, listen to what God has to say about you. He thinks you're pretty terrific, and He knows you can do all kinds of things that you can't even imagine doing at the moment. Let Him build your confidence and just see what happens then. But brace yourself: Not even the sky is the limit where He's concerned!

I Will

	yes	no
Allow God to restore my self-confidence.	___	___
Believe that I can do all things through Christ.	___	___
Pay close attention to God's opinion of me.	___	___
Get rid of anything that hinders my spiritual growth.	___	___
Understand that healthy confidence is not the same as unhealthy conceit.	___	___
Expect God to enable me to do things I can't even imagine.	___	___

Things to Do

☐ Make a list of all the things you could do if you really believed Philippians 4:13.

☐ Hand your self-esteem over to God to make whatever repairs are necessary.

☐ Ask God to forgive you for doubting the abilities He gave you.

☐ Look in a mirror and say, "God thinks I'm terrific!" Then say it again.

☐ Try doing something new—something you used to tell yourself that you couldn't possibly do.

☐ Read Psalm 139.

Things to Remember

Ananias told Saul, "The God of our fathers has chosen you that you should know His will, and see the Just One, and hear the voice of His mouth."

ACTS 22:14 NKJV

As many as are led by the Spirit of God, these are sons of God.

ROMANS 8:14 NKJV

Little children, you are from God, and have conquered them; for the one who is in you is greater than the one who is in the world.

1 JOHN 4:4 NRSV

I can do all things through Christ who strengthens me.

PHILIPPIANS 4:13 NKJV

Paul wrote: I bow my knees to the Father of our Lord Jesus Christ... that He would grant you, according to the riches of His glory, to be strengthened with might through His Spirit in the inner man.

EPHESIANS 3:14 NKJV

We have to take ourselves, good and bad alike, on trust before we can do anything.

MARTIN ISRAEL

A humble knowledge of yourself is a surer way to God than an extensive search after learning.

THOMAS À KEMPIS

REVENGE

Making a Comeback

Beloved, do not avenge yourselves, but rather give place to wrath; for it is written, "Vengeance is Mine, I will repay," says the Lord.

—*Romans 12:19* NKJV

Dave overhears you telling Paul that you've finally worked up the nerve to ask Holly to the prom, and the next thing you know, he goes and asks her first. You can't believe it! Dave, of all people! Well, he's just landed a secure spot on your ex-friend list.

But that's not quite enough; you really want to make him pay for this. You feel like a boxer who's ready to make his comeback after a humiliating defeat. You want your opponent to suffer big-time. Your mind races with devious schemes for getting back at him. Most involve bodily harm—the kind that would keep him out of the way until after prom night. You want revenge, and plenty of it.

The urge to exact revenge is perfectly normal; giving in to that urge is perfectly awful. Whatever satisfaction you may get from it will be so short-lived that you'll wonder why you thought it was such a good idea in the first place. And then you'll begin to feel perfectly miserable.

Instead of exacting revenge, try doing good by offering forgiveness. Until you forgive an offender, your hardened heart—the Bible calls this a "stony" heart—fills up with anger and bitterness—not just toward the offender, but also toward others and even yourself. *Why did I have to go open my big mouth with Dave standing right behind me? Why didn't I ask Holly sooner?* you wonder, beating yourself up by second-guessing. Does this sound like a fun way to live?

Forgiveness heals. When you forgive others, the open wounds they inflict on you begin to close up—and the bruises you give yourself begin to fade. Eventually, the sore spots disappear altogether. And God will make good on His promise to replace your hard and stony heart with a softened heart that beats with new life.

By the way, if you're tempted to suddenly get biblical and start quoting the "eye for an eye" verse from Exodus 21, you might want to know that God intended that to be a standard for the court system, not an excuse for personal retribution. God came right out and laid it on the line: "Vengeance is Mine"—not yours. You want to see vengeance? Nobody can do vengeance like God can. Keep your mitts off the situation, forgive the offender, and let God handle it. He'll do a much better job, and you won't end up feeling perfectly miserable.

I Will

Trust God to handle offenses on my behalf.

_____ yes _____ no

Put the healing power of forgiveness to the test whenever I'm offended.

_____ yes _____ no

Allow God to soften my hard heart.

_____ yes _____ no

Recognize the desire for revenge and squelch it immediately.

_____ yes _____ no

Remember that only God has the authority to seek vengeance.

_____ yes _____ no

Learn to forgive those who hurt me instead of to want revenge.

_____ yes _____ no

Things to Do

 Give your heart of stone to God so He can soften it.

Read Matthew 5:39–45 to see what the Lord expects you to do to avoid exacting revenge.

Read several biblical accounts of revenge that backfired, such as 2 Samuel 3:22–39; 1 Kings 22:24–38; the story of Haman throughout the book of Esther; Ezekiel 25.

There's a saying that suggests you dig two graves before setting out on a journey of revenge. In your journal, write about how this warning can apply to your life.

Memorize Matthew 5:44.

Jesus said, "I say to you, love your enemies, bless those who curse you, do good to those who hate you, and pray for those who spitefully use you and persecute you."

MATTHEW 5:44 NKJV

The LORD said, "I will give you a new heart and put a new spirit within you; I will take the heart of stone out of your flesh and give you a heart of flesh."

EZEKIEL 36:26 NKJV

Do not say, "I will recompense evil;" wait for the LORD, and He will save you.

PROVERBS 20:22 NKJV

Jesus said, "Will not God bring about justice for his chosen ones, who cry out to him day and night? Will he keep putting them off? I tell you, he will see that they get justice, and quickly. However, when the Son of Man comes, will he find faith on the earth?"

LUKE 18:7–8 NIV

See that no one renders evil for evil to anyone, but always pursue what is good both for yourselves and for all.

1 THESSALONIANS 5:15 NKJV

There is no revenge so complete as forgiveness.

JOSH BILLINGS

Never does the human soul appear so strong and noble as when it forgoes revenge and dares to forgive an injury.

EDWIN HUBBEL CHAPIN

CHOOSING YOUR BATTLES

Don't Sweat It

David said to the Philistine, "All this assembly shall know that the Lord does not save with sword and spear; for the battle is the Lord's, and He will give you into our hands."
—*1 Samuel 17:47* NKJV

You've worked hard and trained like a maniac for months. No one has practiced shooting hoops more than you have—even the guys in the neighborhood say you're good at it, and they never say that about a girl! There's one spot left open on the girls' varsity basketball team, and you've claimed that spot for yourself, even if you're only a sophomore.

But when that final roster is announced, you're stunned—you didn't make it! Some junior got the last open slot on the team, and you know why. She just happens to be the daughter of a school board member. Favoritism, that's all it is! Just wait till you get home and tell your parents! That school is in for one big messy fight. Your parents will see to it that you get on the team.

Back away from the edge. Calm down. Take a deep breath and ask yourself a couple of questions: *Is this* really worth fighting for? Will this matter five years from now? Do I want to play basketball—which I can do on the JV team—or do I want to look good by being the only sophomore on the varsity team? If you choose to go ahead with this fight, you're in for a prolonged struggle that will accomplish little besides spreading bad feelings all around. As they say, no good can come from this.

With maturity and wisdom comes the ability to decide what is worth fighting for and what isn't. Some battles are obvious: Anything of eternal value is worth fighting to the death for; a no-brainer is a battle that isn't even worth taking time to think about. But then there are all those battles in between—struggles for personal rights or for important principles like fairness and justice. That's when you have to ask yourself the kinds of questions mentioned above.

So when is a battle worth it? There will be times when only you, with God's guidance, can decide that. If it is worth it, then you need to give it all you've got, to the point where you're willing to suffer whatever consequences result from your efforts—including going to jail or being injured or losing your job. If it's not worth it, don't sweat it. There's no point in wasting your time, energy, and witness for Christ on a struggle over trivial matters. Leave the battle to God and move on with your life.

I Will

Trust God to help me determine what is worth
fighting for and what isn't.   *yes*   *no*

Be willing to walk away from a pointless fight,
even when it hurts to do so.   *yes*   *no*

Have the courage to fight it out when eternal
consequences are at stake.   *yes*   *no*

Keep a cool head no matter what kind of battle
I'm engaged in.   *yes*   *no*

Have a mature attitude toward the battles I face.   *yes*   *no*

Strive to be known as a peacemaker.   *yes*   *no*

Things to Do

 Ask God to reveal to you any areas in your life in which you tend to
make a big deal over trivial issues.

 Memorize Romans 12:17–18.

☐ Copy Norman Vincent Peale's quotation at the top of a journal page and
beneath it write out your thoughts on how a masterly retreat can be a
victory.

☐ Resolve to fight only for those principles and values that are of lasting
or eternal significance.

☐ Cultivate your role as a peacemaker by creating a strategy for resolving
disputes among your friends.

Jesus said, "Love your enemies, do good to those who hate you, bless those who curse you, and pray for those who spitefully use you. To him who strikes you on the one cheek, offer the other also. And from him who takes away your cloak, do not withhold your tunic either."

LUKE 6:27–29 NKJV

Repay no one evil for evil. Have regard for good things in the sight of all men. If it is possible, as much as depends on you, live peaceably with all men.

ROMANS 12:17–18 NKJV

Fight the good fight for the Christian faith, take hold of everlasting life, to which you were called and about which you made a good testimony in front of many witnesses.

1 TIMOTHY 6:12 GOD'S WORD

We do not wrestle against flesh and blood, but against principalities, against powers, against the rulers of the darkness of this age, against spiritual hosts of wickedness in the heavenly places.

EPHESIANS 6:12 NKJV

We live in this world, but we don't act like its people.

2 CORINTHIANS 10:3 CEV

Part of the happiness of life consists not in fighting battles, but in avoiding them. A masterly retreat is in itself a victory.

NORMAN VINCENT PEALE

PEER PRESSURE

The Jury of Your Peers

Be strong in the Lord and in the power of His might.
—Ephesians 6:10 NKJV

Jenna and Cindi hook up with you after school on a Friday afternoon. Everyone's got only one thing on her mind—it's the weekend! You're all free to do as you please! Jenna tells you that she's going to hang out at Cindi's and later go to McDonald's before heading to the movies. "You want to come?" Cindi asks. You can't, you tell them—your mother asked you to come straight home from school today. They roll their eyes and give each other a knowing look. "That's OK," Jenna says. "We'll see if Teresa can come instead."

Hold it—that's not an example of peer pressure, is it? Nobody pressured you into doing anything. Neither Jenna nor Cindi tried to talk you into going with them. They even said it was OK. So how can this situation have anything to do with peer pressure?

Well, maybe you should take another look, because

these two girls have just pulled off a masterful example of the subtle way teenagers exert pressure on each other. They rolled their eyes ("Here we go again—it's always something"), gave each other a knowing look ("Golly gee, we sure have a sweet little obedient girl here, don't we?"), and said they'd ask Teresa "instead" ("You, child, can be replaced, and don't you forget it!"). They stopped just short of calling you a baby and giving you the boot.

And how about you? Once Jenna and Cindi finished doing their number on you, didn't your mind start to work overtime? *Mom didn't say why she wanted me to come home. It's not like we have plans or anything. And besides, it's Friday, and I should be able to do what I want after being cooped up in school all week. And if they start hanging around with Teresa—well, they know Teresa and I don't get along, so I don't want that to happen...* Do you still think you haven't been pressured?

Peer pressure does not have to be heavy-handed to be effective; it can be as subtle as a brief glance passing between two people. It's an incredibly powerful mechanism for getting you to do what someone else wants you to do. It influences the way you walk and talk and dress and behave and spend your time—as well as who you spend your time with. It's manipulation to the max.

Can you see now what you're up against? It's going to take all the strength and discipline you can muster—and a whole lot of quick and silent prayers—to maintain your resolve to do the right thing when your friends lay a peer-pressure trip on you. You need to be "strong in the Lord and in the power of His might"—all the time, day in and day out. There's just no other way. You can try to resist the pressure in your own strength, but there will come a day when you're tired of always being the one who says no, always trying to do the right thing, and you'll no longer have the strength to walk away. Without God's power to support you, you'll simply give in.

The way to plug in to God's power, and stay plugged in, is to first make sure you have a daily routine that includes spending time with Him, in prayer, in the Word, in meditation and reflection. Then you have to go one step further: You need to put on the whole armor of God—the belt of truth, the shoes of the good news about peace, the shield of faith, the helmet of God's saving power, the sword of the Word of God. (You can find a complete description of this armor in Ephesians 6 in the New Testament.)

Only when you leave the house each morning wearing the armor of God can you hope to be prepared for the pressure you will face. The belt will help you recognize deception. The shoes will remind you to share—and live by—the gospel. The shield will keep doubt at bay. The helmet will assure you of your standing with God. And the sword—your one offensive weapon—will slice through your enemy's cagey attempts to keep you from obeying God. The armor of God is critical—don't leave home without it!

I Will

Put on the armor of God before I leave the house each morning.

yes _no_

Trust God to help me resist the temptation to go along with the crowd.

yes _no_

Learn to recognize both the subtle and overt ways teenagers pressure each other.

yes _no_

Make every effort to avoid placing the wrong kind of pressure on my friends.

yes _no_

Be aware that peer pressure will extend even into my adult years.

yes _no_

Things to Do

☐ Peer pressure existed even in Jesus' time. Read the scriptures that follow to find out who was exerting the pressure.

☐ Memorize Proverbs 4:14–15 and 3 John 1:1.

☐ Thank God in advance for helping you stand strong in the face of peer pressure.

☐ Write a letter to an imaginary (or real) friend who is feeling pressured to do drugs. Explain how he or she can resist the pressure.

☐ Read Ephesians 6:10–18 and come up with a way to remind yourself to put on the whole armor of God each day.

Things to Remember

Do not enter the path of the wicked, and do not walk in the way of evil. Avoid it, do not travel on it; turn away from it and pass on.

PROVERBS 4:14–15 NKJV

Paul wrote: Many live as enemies of the cross of Christ; I have often told you of them, and now I tell you even with tears. Their end is destruction, their god is the belly, and their glory is in their shame; their minds are set on earthly things.

PHILIPPIANS 3:18–19 NRSV

Do not imitate what is evil, but what is good. He who does good is of God, but he who does evil has not seen God.

—3 JOHN 1:11 NKJV

There was much complaining among the people concerning Him. Some said, "He is good"; others said, "No, on the contrary, He deceives the people." However, no one spoke openly of Him for fear of the Jews.

JOHN 7:12–13 NKJV

Nevertheless even among the rulers many believe in Him, but because of the Pharisees they did now confess Him, lest they be put out of the synagogue; for they loved the praise of men more than the praise of God.

JOHN 12:42–43 NKJV

His parents answered them and said, "We know that this is our son, and that he was born blind; but by what means he now sees we do not know . . . He is of age; ask him. He will speak for himself." His parents said these things because they feared the Jews, for the Jews had agreed already that if anyone confessed that He was Christ, he would be put out of the synagogue.

JOHN 9:20–22 NKJV

Pilate sought to release Him, but the Jews cried out, saying, "If you let this Man go, you are not Caesar's friend. Whoever makes himself a king speaks against Caesar." When Pilate therefore heard that saying, he brought Jesus out and sat down in the judgment seat in a place that is called The Pavement, but in Hebrew, Gabbatha.

JOHN 19:12–13 NKJV

The things which you learned and received and heard and saw in me, these do, and the God of peace will be with you.

PHILIPPIANS 4:9 NKJV

I have forgiven that one for your sakes in the presence of Christ, lest Satan should take advantage of us; for we are not ignorant of his devices.

2 CORINTHIANS 2:10–11 NKJV

Character is always lost when a high ideal is sacrificed on the altar of conformity and popularity.

—AUTHOR UNKNOWN

The opposite of bravery is not cowardice but conformity.

—ROBERT ANTHONY

Endless Possibilities

I know the thoughts that I think toward you, says the LORD, thoughts of peace and not of evil, to give you a future and a hope.

—*Jeremiah 29:11* NKJV

What do you say when the zillionth person asks what your plans are for the future? Maybe you have a specific goal in life, so your plans naturally line up with that goal; you want to be a doctor, so you know you'll be going to medical school. Perhaps you're not sure exactly what you want to do, but you have several ideas in mind, possibly social work or teaching; either one will require a college degree, so you decide to take some basic courses at first until you can refine your goals. If you're joining the family business, well, your path is pretty obvious to everyone.

Or maybe you're like Nick. He developed an elaborate plan for his life, starting with four years of college and then law school, spending each summer on the mission field. Then he'd marry and wait two years before having children. Nick has overhauled his plan three times since high school, and he's now taking courses at a community college while he figures out what to do with his life!

Making plans for the future is tricky business, that's for sure. You can't predict the future, but you can't ignore it either. And then there's the not-so-small matter of God's will to consider. So where do you start? That depends on whether you want to let God lead or you want to go your own way, hiding your crossed fingers behind your back. If you let God lead, all you have to do is follow. If you go your own way, you have to hope and pray that God will bless your plans and bail you out when things go wrong.

When you allow God to set your course, you lay your future before Him and let Him order your steps. Your willingness to follow Him delights the Father so much that He will give you every opportunity to reach your goal. He'll open doors for you that no one else could open—and He'll close those doors that you should not walk through. He'll give you possibilities for your future that you can't even imagine today.

Meanwhile, what answer can you give your questioner that makes sense in the current economic climate and the future job market and all that? Tell the truth: Your divine Dad is helping you plan your future—and no one knows the future like He does.

I Will

Consult God before making any plans for my life. _____ yes _____ no

Relax in the knowledge that God will not steer me
in the wrong direction. _____ yes _____ no

Learn to recognize the signs that indicate I'm on
the right track. _____ yes _____ no

Be thankful that I have help in sorting
out my future. _____ yes _____ no

Be open to whatever God has in store for me. _____ yes _____ no

Remember that only God knows the future. _____ yes _____ no

Things to Do

☐ Ask God what His plans are for your life.

☐ Listen for His answer.

☐ Memorize Jeremiah 29:11.

☐ Set aside a page in your journal where you can write down those things
that God reveals to you about His plan.

☐ Come up with an appropriate answer to give those who ask about your
plans, and be prepared to gently defend your decision to trust God.

☐ Decide what you can do today that fits in to God's plan for your life.

Things to Remember

Commit your way to the LORD, trust also in Him, and He shall bring it to pass.

PSALM 37:5 NKJV

Jesus said, "When [the shepherd] brings out his own sheep, he goes before them, and the sheep follow him, for they know his voice."

JOHN 10:4 NKJV

Let them do good, that they be rich in good works, ready to give, willing to share, storing up for themselves a good foundation for the time to come, that they may lay hold on eternal life.

1 TIMOTHY 6:18–19 NKJV

There is laid up for me the crown of righteousness, which the Lord, the righteous Judge, will give to me on that Day, and not to me only but also to all who have loved His appearing.

2 TIMOTHY 4:8 NKJV

. . . .

Plan for this world as if you expect to live forever; but plan for the hereafter as if you expect to die tomorrow.

IBN GABIROL

Expect the best, plan for the worst, and prepare to be surprised.

DENIS WAITLEY

CHOICES

Gray Matters

Your ears shall hear a word behind you, saying, "This is the way, walk in it." Whenever you turn to the right hand or whenever you turn to the left.

—*Isaiah 30:21* NKJV

Your parents, who think your schedule is overloaded, give you an ultimatum—give up your spot on the cheerleading squad or quit volunteering at the public library. You love to do both: Cheerleading keeps you physically fit, and working at the library keeps you mentally fit. What should you do?

The youth pastor just posted a list of summer missions opportunities: Help build low-income housing with Habitat for Humanity, assist with Vacation Bible School, join a team sharing the gospel at the beach, or do yard work for disabled people. You would like doing all of these projects, but you'll only have one week off before you start your summer job. Which project will you choose?

Your best friend's parents have just invited you to join their family on a vacation to Mexico. But the trip conflicts with the timing of a special college-level course that would just about seal your admission to the university you want to attend. You can't do both—but both would broaden your experience. How can you possibly decide between the two?

Many choices are easy. Should you do drugs or do God? Watch an X-rated video or walk out of the room? Steal a CD or pay for it? You know the right choice in those situations. But how about when it's not a question of right or wrong, when the options seem more or less equal? You need some solid guidance and a healthy dose of wisdom.

As with everything, the first step you should take is to consult with God. Consider the pros and cons of each option you have, as well as the short- and long-range consequences of your decision. Consider, too, your heart's desire; you can often trust your heart, but only if it is totally surrendered to God. Take into account the seriousness of the situation; in less important situations, one decision may be just as good as another, while other circumstances may require the godly counsel of your parents, teachers, or pastor.

In those gray areas of life, a wrong decision may be uncomfortable but is usually not life-shattering. If you realize you've made the wrong choice, reverse it if possible. Learn from your mistakes. Don't get down on yourself. Think back to the decision-making process you used and revise it the next time you have a tricky choice to make. And always listen for that voice that says, "This is the way, walk in it."

I Will

Consult with God first.   *yes*   *no*

Think carefully about where each choice I make
may take me.   *yes*   *no*

Consider the long- and short-range consequences
of my choices.   *yes*   *no*

Realize that I cannot leave significant decisions
to chance.   *yes*   *no*

Trust my heart only if it is completely
surrendered to God.   *yes*   *no*

Things to Do

 Make the best decision: Decide now that you will consult with God first whenever you're confronted with a major decision.

Read *Life on the Edge* by James Dobson, a book designed to help teens make the right choices.

Memorize Isaiah 30:21.

Develop a decision-making strategy for the gray areas in life. Write it down.

Recall the last time you made a bad decision—a real whopper. See what you can learn from that situation.

Trust in the LORD with all your heart, and lean not on your own understanding; in all your ways acknowledge Him, and He shall direct your paths.

PROVERBS 3:5–6 NKJV

I will instruct you and teach you in the way you should go; I will guide you with My eye.

PSALM 32:8 NKJV

The steps of a good man are ordered by the LORD, and He delights in his way.

PSALM 37:23 NKJV

Moses said, "The LORD, He is the One who goes before you. He will be with you, He will not leave you nor forsake you; do not fear nor be dismayed."

DEUTERONOMY 31:8 NKJV

Where there is no counsel, the people fall; but in the multitude of counselors there is safety.

PROVERBS 11:14 NKJV

Every choice you make has an end result.

ZIG ZIGLAR

The man or woman who is wholly or joyously surrendered to Christ can't make a wrong choice—any choice will be the right one.

A. W. TOZER

Cutting Loose

Our mouth was filled with laughter, and our tongue with singing. Then they said among the nations, "The LORD has done great things for them." —*Psalm 126:2 NKJV*

Most people don't have to be reminded to laugh. You probably have genuinely funny friends who come up with such great wisecracks that even the teachers have to laugh. Unless you're telling mean-spirited jokes at someone else's expense, laughter hardly seems to be a spiritual issue. So why talk about "cutting loose"? If anything, people act as if you never take life seriously enough as it is!

Maybe you do need to take life more seriously. Just don't take yourself too seriously in the process. The ability to laugh at yourself—with all your weaknesses and foibles and missteps—gives you a healthy and balanced perspective that will carry you through many awkward situations in your life. When you can make light of an embarrassing performance in which you are the red-faced star, you put everyone at ease, especially yourself. You've probably already witnessed a scenario like that: The principal or the pastor or a guest speaker in an assembly program makes an incredibly stupid mistake. Everyone seems to hold their breath until the "star" cracks a joke about his gaffe. You can actually hear everyone start to breathe again, can't you?

Cutting loose does carry a set of rules, though. Never, ever demean yourself. When you laugh at yourself in a derogatory way, it makes everyone around you uncomfortable, and it diminishes the value that God places on your life. You end up feeling worse than you did when you made the original mistake, which is exactly the opposite of what you're trying to accomplish. You want to feel better about the situation, right? So keep it light, and find the humor in the "humanness" of all those things you do that you think make you look foolish. Realize that they just make you look human.

God gave you the gift of laughter to balance out the problems that will come into your life, just as they come into everyone's life. Look at the older people you know: The ones with a twinkle in their eye are those who have learned to use the gift of laughter wisely. They've developed a sense of humor that lets them take the garbage Satan has tried to dump on them and fling it back in his face. (Imagine how he'd look with rotten leftovers from a broken Hefty bag dripping all over him.)

Delight in the things God intended you to delight in. Make light of your blunders and cherish the joy of laughter. Cut loose—and go live the abundant life.

I Will

Honor God by having a balanced perspective on
who I am.   _____ yes   _____ no

Delight in the life God has given me.   _____ yes   _____ no

Understand the difference between laughing at
myself in a healthy way and degrading myself. _____ yes   _____ no

Make light of the mistakes I make.   _____ yes   _____ no

Put others at ease with my sense of humor.   _____ yes   _____ no

Refuse to participate in mean-spirited jokes. _____ yes   _____ no

Things to Do

☐ Watch your favorite sitcom or comedy and take note of how much of
the humor is degrading.

☐ Ask God to make you sensitive to any kind of joking that could hurt
someone else.

☐ Read Job 8:1–21 to see how repentance can lead to laughter.

☐ Learn about the health benefits of laughter.

☐ Check out one of the many Christian humor books, like Bible Humor:
Top Seven Lists by David Veerman and Rich Anderson.

☐ Visit the Fellowship of Merry Christians at
www.joyfulnoiseletter.com.

Jesus said, "Blessed are you who hunger now, for you shall be filled. Blessed are you who weep now, for you shall laugh."

LUKE 6:21 NKJV

Light shines on the godly, and joy on those who do right.

PSALM 97:11 NLT

He will yet fill your mouth with laughing, and your lips with rejoicing.

JOB 8:21 NKJV

A merry heart makes a cheerful countenance, but by sorrow of the heart the spirit is broken.

PROVERBS 15:13 NKJV

And Sarah said, "God has made me laugh, and all who hear will laugh with me."

GENESIS 21:6 NKJV

The LORD said, "Then out of them shall proceed thanksgiving and the voice of those who make merry; I will multiply them, and they shall not diminish; I will also glorify them, and they shall not be small."

JEREMIAH 30:19 NKJV

. . . .

Hearty laughter is a good way to jog internally without having to go outdoors.

NORMAN COUSINS

LISTENING

Body Language

---

*Let every man be swift to hear, slow to speak,
slow to wrath.*

—James 1:19 NKJV

You stare at the test you've just been handed and wonder what on earth it's about. Uh-oh. The test is based on what your teacher said in class. Big problem. *Oh, why didn't I take notes?* you think.

You're riding home from church with your parents, and all they can talk about is how great the sermon was. Huh? *What's she talking about?* It sure didn't sound like anything special to you.

Then you get home, and your dad says, "Just once I wish you'd listen to me and quit leaving your stuff all over the house." *What's he talking about?* you wonder.

Good listening skills don't seem to come naturally, do they? How can you activate your hearing?

Listen with your hands. Get in the habit of taking notes. As you go through life, you'll discover that even once you're out of school—whether high school or college—you'll find yourself in countless situations that require note-taking.

Listen with your spirit. Expect God to speak to you every time you hear a sermon, a testimony, a Christian television or radio program, or a Christian CD. You can activate your spirit by asking God to reveal to you what He wants you to get out of the message, and that in turn activates your hearing.

Listen with your actions. Productive listening requires action. When your dad says he wishes you'd listen to him, he means he wants you to obey him—not just hear his words accurately. The same principle holds for spiritual listening. James 1:22 tells believers to be "doers of the word, and not hearers only."

Listen with your mouth. It's been said that God gave you two ears and one mouth because He wants you to listen twice as much as you talk. But you can "listen" by asking the right questions at the right time.

Listen with your eyes. In every situation, you'd do well to discipline yourself to look at the person speaking to you. That goes for your teacher, your pastor, your parents, and anyone you have a conversation with.

Above all, learn to look at God when He speaks to you. Keep your focus on Him. Let Him know that you care about what He's saying to you, that you not only believe Him and believe in Him but you also have every intention of acting on what He tells you to do. Then go out and do it.

I Will

Expect God to speak to me.

_____ yes   _____ no

Show my love for God by giving Him my
wholehearted attention.

_____ yes   _____ no

Make sure that I am a doer of the Word and not just
a hearer.

_____ yes   _____ no

Learn what it means to activate my hearing.

_____ yes   _____ no

Listen twice as much as I speak.

_____ yes   _____ no

Show respect by paying attention when
someone is talking.

_____ yes   _____ no

Things to Do

☐ Ask God to speak to you through a message given by your pastor or
youth leader.

☐ Take notes during the next sermon you hear. If you're already in the
habit, try to take better notes.

☐ Learn to recognize "action points" — practical things you can do — by
consciously listening for them the next time you hear a sermon or other
message.

☐ Make a commitment to God that you will do what you have heard Him
tell you to do.

☐ Pay close attention to the way people listen to you tomorrow. Write
down what you appreciated and what annoyed you about their behavior.

Jesus said to them, "He who has ears to hear, let him hear!"

MARK 4:9 NKJV

Jesus said, "He who has an ear, let him hear what the Spirit says to the churches."

REVELATION 2:29 NKJV

Moses said, "Because you have listened to the voice of the LORD your God, to keep all His commandments which I command you today, to do what is right in the eyes of the LORD your God."

DEUTERONOMY 13:18 NKJV

David wrote: Come, you children, listen to me; I will teach you the fear of the LORD.

PSALM 34:11 NKJV

The LORD said, "Oh, that My people would listen to Me, that Israel would walk in My ways!"

PSALM 81:13 NKJV

. . . .

Listening, not imitation, may be the sincerest form of flattery.

JOYCE BROTHERS

The greatest gift you can give another is the purity of your attention.

RICHARD MOSS

Who's the Boss?

Whatever you do, do it heartily, as to the Lord and not to men, knowing that from the Lord you will receive the reward of the inheritance; for you serve the Lord Christ.
—*Colossians 3:23–24* NKJV

Say you come home from school one day and there's no food in the house—nothing at all. You think, *This is it. I'm going to die, right here and now. I'm starving!* Physical weakness begins to overtake you. You lie on the sofa, stricken by the fate that has befallen you. All this, and you've only been home for twenty minutes.

You hear your mom's van pull in the driveway, and hope begins to stir deep within you. She must have gone to the supermarket. You look out the window—it's even better than that! She's carrying two huge pizza boxes, and your kid sister is carrying a third box. "Sorry, Son," your mother says, as you lunge toward one of the boxes before they can even get in the house. "You can't have any."

What? What?? Calmly, she quotes the end of 2 Thessalonians 3:10: "If anyone will not work, neither shall he eat." *Gulp*. She nailed you, and nailed you good. All week she had been asking you to help with one thing or another, but you kept putting her off. Last weekend she and your sister cleaned out the garage while you holed up in your room. Unfortunately, your behavior over the past week was not unusual—you always seem to find some excuse to get out of helping.

Looks like your day of reckoning has come. If you want to eat again, you'd better get to work. And you'd better get used to the reality that work is not an option, because that's a fact you'll be living with for the rest of your days on earth.

The Bible is very clear about the importance of work—so clear that it calls a person who refuses to work a whole host of crummy names, especially in the book of Proverbs. God designed people to be productive, and He designed work to be an essential factor in shaping a person's life. Your satisfaction in life is so closely tied to the work you do—to your contribution to your family and the community—that the stronger your work ethic is, the more content you'll be.

Maybe you find that hard to swallow right now; work is a four-letter word that you've managed to avoid. Meanwhile, your helpful little sister, Mom's willing worker, finds it pretty easy to swallow, right along with a couple of slices of pepperoni pizza. With extra cheese. And sausage.

I Will

Understand that God designed me to be a productive person.

_____ yes   _____ no

Ask God to make me a willing worker.

_____ yes   _____ no

Pitch in and help around the house.

_____ yes   _____ no

Realize that work is not an option in life.

_____ yes   _____ no

View work as a factor in shaping my life and providing lifelong satisfaction.

_____ yes   _____ no

Develop a strong work ethic.

_____ yes   _____ no

Things to Do

☐ Read through the book of Proverbs, listing all the verses that refer to work or idleness, for an indication of how seriously God views work.

☐ Ask God to show you how you can become a more willing worker.

☐ Make a list of little and big things that you know need to be done around the house. Commit yourself to helping to get those jobs done.

☐ Memorize Colossians 3:23–24 and remember it the next time you have a job to do.

☐ Pretend that you own a business—something you're familiar with, like a retail store. Write down the qualities you'd like in an employee. Concentrate on developing those qualities in your own character.

Let the beauty of the LORD our God be upon us, and establish the work of our hands for us; yes, establish the work of our hands.

PSALM 90:17 NKJV

Nothing is better for a man than that he should eat and drink, and that his soul should enjoy good in his labor. This also, I saw, was from the hand of God.

ECCLESIASTES 2:24 NKJV

Even when we were with you, we commanded you this: If anyone will not work, neither shall he eat.

2 THESSALONIANS 3:10 NKJV

Let him who stole steal no longer, but rather let him labor, working with his hands what is good, that he may have something to give him who has need.

EPHESIANS 4:28 NKJV

Jesus said to His disciples, "The harvest truly is plentiful, but the laborers are few. Therefore pray the Lord of the harvest to send out laborers into His harvest."

MATTHEW 9:37–38 NKJV

Work for the fun of it, and the money will arrive some day.

RONNIE MILSAP

In case of doubt, do a little more than you have to.

WARREN MITCHELL

The Real Thing

As the deer pants for the water brooks, so pants my soul for You, O God.

—Psalm 42:1 NKJV

A woman you know considers herself a highly spiritual person. She meditates and chants and does some sort of thing with crystals and believes in the healing power of a rock. Meanwhile, the witch down the block—no, not some mean old crab but a real, live, bona fide witch—claims to have found true spirituality in wicca. Your whole family is born-again, and that's supposed to make them spiritual. What gives? How can they all believe they're spiritual?

Spirituality involves those things that nurture your spirit. Because you are a spiritual being, you need to "feed" your spirit in order to be spiritually strong, just as you need to feed your body in order to have physical strength. As a Christian, you've no doubt discovered that the only real way to find true spirituality is through reading the Word of God and cultivating an intimate relationship with the Father through Jesus Christ. In fact, genuine spirituality simply means becoming more Christlike by spending time in His presence.

Other people, like the rock-healer and the witch, often recognize their spiritual nature and sense the need to nurture it. Some openly reject Christ and turn to other gods, but many seek fulfillment in a variety of rituals and philosophies and beliefs only because they've never heard about Jesus—or because what they've heard bears little resemblance to the truth. The apostle Paul understood the spiritual nature of those who worshiped other gods and looked for love in all the wrong places. Instead of criticizing them, he appealed to their spirituality and opened their eyes to the reality of the one true God. Society today is a lot like it was in Paul's day, with so many varieties of religious belief. If you want to be an effective witness, you'd do well to follow Paul's example by acknowledging—and respecting—the spiritual need that causes people to seek other gods in the first place.

If you have had a life-changing encounter with Jesus, you know the hunger deep down inside of you that wants more of Him and less of you. You can try to ignore the hunger by filling up with empty activities, but the hunger never disappears. Nurture your spirit by getting closer to God. Immerse yourself in His presence. Seek to be more Christlike. Fill your mind and heart with God's Word. Your spiritual strength will witness to those whose hunger has yet to lead them to the real thing—Jesus Christ.

I Will

Trust God to keep me from being deceived by
false spirituality.

yes _____ _no_ _____

Nurture my spirit by spending time with God and
His Word.

yes _____ _no_ _____

Place a high priority on building up my spiritual
strength.

yes _____ _no_ _____

Seek to become more Christlike.

yes _____ _no_ _____

Acknowledge the spirituality in those who do not
believe as I do.

yes _____ _no_ _____

Things to Do

 Make it your number one goal to become more Christlike. Write it down,
date it, and sign it.

☐ Read how Paul appealed to the spirituality of unbelievers in Acts
17:23–27.

☐ List the varieties of belief that you've encountered in your community.
Use Paul's example to create a script to lead adherents of those beliefs
to Christ.

☐ Come up with a daily "meal plan" for nurturing your spirit (such as a
certain number of "helpings" of prayer, Bible verses, and so forth).

 Ask God to keep you from trying to satisfy your spiritual hunger with
empty activities.

On the last day, that great day of the feast, Jesus stood and cried out, saying, "If anyone thirsts, let him come to Me and drink. He who believes in Me, as the Scripture has said, out of his heart will flow rivers of living water."

JOHN 7:37–38 NKJV

Jesus said, "'You shall love the Lord your God with all your heart, with all your soul, with all your mind, and with all your strength.' This is the first commandment."

MARK 12:30 NKJV

Jesus said, "The thief does not come except to steal, and to kill, and to destroy. I have come that they may have life, and that they may have it more abundantly."

JOHN 10:10 NKJV

Oh, taste and see that the LORD is good; blessed is the man who trusts in Him.

PSALM 34:8 NKJV

You are not a human being in search of a spiritual experience. You are a spiritual being immersed in a human experience.

PIERRE TEILHARD DE CHARDIN

When you examine the lives of the most influential people who have ever walked among us, you discover one thread that winds through them all. They have been aligned first with their spiritual nature and only then with their physical selves.

ALBERT EINSTEIN

Mastermind

Those who are Christ's have crucified the flesh with its passions and desires.

—*Galatians 5:24* NKJV

Crucify the flesh? Did you really read the verse above? You know what crucifixion is, and you know it isn't pretty. What's more, it's a killer. So now the Bible is telling you to kill your body? If that's what you think that means, then you need to understand what the Bible means when it refers to "the flesh." Your flesh is that part of you that gives rise to sinful "passions and desires," as Paul wrote to the Galatians. Your flesh is in a constant battle with your spirit, the part of you that strives to live in a godly way.

If you belong to Christ, your flesh has already been crucified—so avoiding sin should be a piece of cake, right? No, because you still have to deal with Satan, who tries to break down your self-control by becoming the master of your mind, knowing that your thoughts determine your actions. The Bible depicts him as one sneaky creature, prowling about, looking to devour weak believers. Remember, too, that just because he doesn't get you on the "big" sins, that doesn't mean he's defeated. You also need to crucify the flesh by exercising control over any bad habit you have, whether it's eating too many snack cakes or talking on the phone too much or passing notes in class.

You continue to crucify the flesh as you set your mind on the things of the Spirit. You won't be walking around like some haloed saint in a medieval painting, but your awareness of God will become so acute that you will want to do His will instead of satisfying your own desires. You can discipline your body, mind, and spirit to bring honor to His name by not giving in to sinful desire or seemingly innocent addictions, like absolutely having to watch every episode of Friends or buying every teen magazine that even briefly mentions 'N Sync. As one of the nine qualities known as the fruit of the Spirit, self-control shows others that you are a Spirit-controlled believer.

Each time you exercise self-control you grow stronger in the Lord and become more confident in your ability to ward off Satan's future efforts at devouring you. Each time you exercise self-control you also invite peace to settle over your life as you avoid the guilt that comes from knowing you've given in to wrong. Finally, each time you exercise self-control you confirm the high regard you place on maintaining a right relationship with the Father—and that pleases Him to no end.

I Will

Be thankful for the trust God has in me to do the
right thing.

_____ yes   _____ no

Rely on God to help me control myself.

_____ yes   _____ no

Learn to see the valuable outcome of discipline,
no matter how painful it is.

_____ yes   _____ no

Be aware of the need to control habitual problems
(such as excessive phone use).

_____ yes   _____ no

Avoid people and circumstances that I know tend
to weaken my resistance to wrongdoing.

_____ yes   _____ no

Things to Do

☐ Meditate on what it means to crucify the flesh.

☐ Think of a time when you were most disciplined, such as when you were
training for a sport or taking music or dance lessons. Apply the
principles you learned then to your personal life now.

☐ Determine your greatest area of indulgence (such as eating). Ask God to
help you control that one area for the next week.

☐ Keep a record of your progress for a week.

☐ List concrete objects that represent areas you need to control (like a
television or computer). Put each one in its place by announcing that
you are superior to it and from now on, you're in control.

Things to Remember

Be on your guard and stay awake. Your enemy, the devil, is like a roaring lion, sneaking around to find someone to attack.

1 Peter 5:8 cev

No discipline is enjoyable while it is happening—it is painful! But afterward there will be a quiet harvest of right living for those who are trained in this way.

Hebrews 12:11 nlt

God wants us to turn from godless living and sinful pleasures and to live good, God-fearing lives day after day.

Titus 2:12 tlb

I will set nothing wicked before my eyes; I hate the work of those who fall away; it shall not cling to me.

Psalm 101:3 nkjv

For this very reason, giving all diligence, add to your faith virtue, to virtue knowledge, to knowledge self-control, to self-control perseverance, to perseverance godliness, to godliness brotherly kindness, and to brotherly kindness love.

2 Peter 1:5–7 nkjv

. . . .

Such power there is in clear-eyed self-restraint.

James Russell Lowell

He who reigns within himself and rules passions, desires, and fears is more than a king.

John Milton

KINDNESS AND COMPASSION

"Now Be Nice"

---

*As the elect of God, holy and beloved, put on tender
mercies, kindness, humility, meekness, longsuffering.*

—*Colossians 3:12* NKJV

Don't you wish you had a dollar for every time your
mother told you to be nice? Hopefully, she doesn't have to
say that to you anymore, but you probably heard it a lot
when you were younger—especially on your way to visit
relatives. Now that you're older, you might wonder about
this whole "nice" business, and with good reason: God
never tells you to be nice. He tells you to be kind. And the
difference between the two is subtle but significant.

Nice is polite; kind is caring, compassionate, and
considerate. Nice is superficial; kind is deep, intense, and
profound. Kindness is a condition of the heart; a kind
person never has to be told, "Now be kind." Compassion
is so much a part of their nature that they simply cannot
turn away from a person who is suffering. Like Mother
Teresa, they see Jesus in every person they meet. To
reject any human being is to reject God Himself.

Becoming a compassionate person is not something you can accomplish by following a well-ordered plan. It stems from a deep and abiding understanding of the compassion Jesus felt for those who were crying out for a Savior—the One who could heal them of diseases, deliver them from demons, and lead them from deception. Needy, helpless people surrounded Him and followed Him wherever He went. His deep love for them moved Him to not only meet their needs but also to empower His disciples to continue His work after He returned to the Father. And He promises to impart to you His love for suffering people just as He imparted it to the disciples.

As your heart fills with compassion, you will become more aware than ever of the tremendous need in the people around you. Keep in mind that it's not just the poor, the hungry, and the homeless who could use a strong dose of the love of Jesus. It's anyone who is hurting or needy, for any reason at all. Could you become the eyes for an elderly woman who is losing her sight? A big sister to an at-risk child who is fresh out of role models? A mechanic for a single mother whose car balks at getting her to work every day?

The simplest act of kindness becomes an extraordinary blessing when God's Spirit is involved. Allow His Spirit to move your heart with compassion, and then follow His lead. Your actions could very well have eternal consequences.

I Will

Meditate on the love and compassion Jesus had for the suffering people around Him.

yes _no_

Be sensitive to the needs of people I know as well as people around the world.

yes _no_

Exchange my niceness for a genuine and healthy helping of compassion.

yes _no_

See Jesus in every person I meet.

yes _no_

Be agreeable, sympathetic, and empathetic toward others.

yes _no_

Things to Do

☐ Read the story of the Good Samaritan in Luke 10:30–37.

☐ Ask God to fill your heart with compassion.

☐ Find out more about the work Mother Teresa did in India—and what kept her going in the midst of horrible and unfathomable circumstances.

☐ List some things you could do as anonymous acts of kindness for people in your community.

☐ Make a list of people in your school and church who could benefit from your help.

☐ Read Burn by Brian Shipman, a book for teens about compassion.

Pure and undefiled religion before God and the Father is this: to visit orphans and widows in their trouble, and to keep oneself unspotted from the world.

JAMES 1:27 NKJV

By purity, by knowledge, by longsuffering, by kindness, by the Holy Spirit, by sincere love.

2 CORINTHIANS 6:6 NKJV

When He saw the multitudes, He was moved with compassion for them, because they were weary and scattered, like sheep having no shepherd.

MATTHEW 9:36 NKJV

The fruit of the Spirit is love, joy, peace, longsuffering, kindness, goodness, faithfulness, gentleness, self-control. Against such there is no law.

GALATIANS 5:22–23 NKJV

Be kind to one another, tenderhearted, forgiving one another, even as God in Christ forgave you.

EPHESIANS 4:32 NKJV

Man may dismiss compassion from his heart, but God never will.

WILLIAM COWPER

Biblical orthodoxy without compassion is surely the ugliest thing in the world.

FRANCIS SCHAEFFER

All Grown Up

Let us go on to perfection, not laying again the foundation of repentance from dead works and of faith toward God.
— *Hebrews 6:1 NKJV*

This is it. Your moment has arrived. It's time to move on, to leave your adolescence behind and accept the responsibility that everyone has told you will come. How will you know that this is your day? Will you rely on the government's assessment? The state may declare you an adult at age eighteen, granting you a dazzling array of rights and privileges. But does that mean that you're now mature—or perfect, as some Bible versions translate the word? No way.

The day you recognize the need to accept responsibility for your life is the day you take your single biggest step toward maturity. You can do that right now, regardless of your age. Start with some very practical steps, like assuming responsibility for doing your own laundry or cleaning up after yourself when you take a shower or have a snack. Keep track of your own appointments. Give your parents plenty of notice when you need to buy something extra for school or you need a ride somewhere. These are small steps, but they can make a big difference.

There are other areas in your life in which you can actively work your way toward greater maturity. You already know one way: taking responsibility for your own actions and words. You can also take specific steps that will help you mature spiritually. Do you have a solid grounding in the basics of your faith? Then it's time to go on to some serious Bible study. It's also time to go deeper in prayer, trusting God to do above and beyond what you can even imagine. How about evangelism? Are you ready to take on more responsibility for sharing the gospel with others? Then there's teaching—can you help teach young children in a Sunday school class? Maybe it's time for you to start a Christian group at school or organize a special youth rally for Christ.

All these actions will help you mature in your faith, because each one requires a deeper dependency on God. You cannot expect to succeed when you take on this kind of responsibility unless you rely on God. Every spiritual activity you perform is another brick in the building of faith that you are creating.

You can keep on adding years to your age without ever moving an inch toward maturity. Or you can gradually take on more responsibility and in the process mature well beyond your years. Which will it be?

I Will

Expect God to help me as I take each step toward greater maturity.

yes *no*

Recognize the need to accept responsibility for my life.

yes *no*

Take on more responsibilities at home.

yes *no*

Realize that my age has nothing to do with my maturity.

yes *no*

Actively work toward maturing spiritually.

yes *no*

Learn to rely on God for increasingly bigger things.

yes *no*

Things to Do

☐ Write in your journal about the relationship between responsibility and maturity.

☐ Make a commitment to gradually accept more responsibility in all areas of your life.

☐ Choose one task, such as doing your own laundry, that you can take on immediately.

☐ Seek suggestions from your pastor or youth leader for a meaty Bible study that would be appropriate for you.

☐ Find out how you can help out with the younger children at church.

Things to Remember

Do not be children in understanding; however, in malice, be babes, but in understanding be mature.

1 CORINTHIANS 14:20 NKJV

Everyone who partakes only of milk is unskilled in the word of righteousness, for he is a babe. But solid food belongs to those who are of full age, that is, those who by reason of use have their senses exercised to discern both good and evil.

HEBREWS 5:13–14 NKJV

Till we all come to the unity of the faith and of the knowledge of the Son of God, to a perfect man, to the measure of the stature of the fullness of Christ; that we should no longer be children, tossed to and fro and carried about with every wind of doctrine, by the trickery of men, in the cunning craftiness of deceitful plotting.

EPHESIANS 4:13–14 NKJV

Him we preach, warning every man and teaching every man in all wisdom, that we may present every man perfect in Christ Jesus.

COLOSSIANS 1:28 NKJV

In the last analysis, the individual person is responsible for living his own life and for "finding himself." If he persists in shifting his responsibility to somebody else, he fails to find out the meaning of his own existence.

THOMAS MERTON

Other Books in the Checklist for Life Series

Checklist for Life
ISBN 0-4852-6455-8

Checklist for Life for Women
ISBN 0-4852-6462-0

Checklist for Life for Men
ISBN 0-4852-6463-9